TIDES AND FLOODS

NEW RESEARCH ON LONDON AND THE TIDAL THAMES FROM THE MIDDLE AGES TO THE TWENTIETH CENTURY

TIDES AND FLOODS
NEW RESEARCH ON LONDON AND THE TIDAL THAMES FROM THE MIDDLE AGES TO THE TWENTIETH CENTURY

A collection of working papers given at the conference 'London, the Thames and water: new historical perspectives', organised by the Centre for Metropolitan History and supported by the Economic and Social Research Council, 16 October 2009

Edited by

James A. Galloway

Centre for Metropolitan History
Working Papers Series, No. 4

Published by
Centre for Metropolitan History
Institute of Historical Research

2010

First published in the United Kingdom in 2010 by

Centre for Metropolitan History
Institute of Historical Research · School of Advanced Study · University of London
Senate House · Malet Street · London WC1E 7HU

ISBN: 978 1 905165 59 9

:

Cover illustration:
A section from 'River Thames with the Docks from Woolwich to the Tower' from
*A Dictionary, Practical, Theoretical, and Historical, of Commerce and Commercial
Navigation* by J.R. McCulloch (London, 1882).

Printed by Lightning Source UK Ltd, 6 Precedent Drive, Rooksley,
Milton Keynes, MK13 8PR

Contents

List of figures and tables

TABLES

List of abbreviations

BA	Bidston Archive, Liverpool World Museum, National Museums and Galleries on Merseyside
BL	British Library
FROG	Foreshore Recording and Observation Group
GLHER	Greater London Historic Environment Record
LCC	London County Council
LMA	London Metropolitan Archives, London
LTI	Liverpool Tidal Institute
LUA	Liverpool University Archive, Liverpool University Sidney Jones Library, Liverpool
MoH	Ministry of Health
MoLA	Museum of London Archaeology
OD	Ordnance Datum
TDP	Thames Discovery Programme
TNA	The National Archives, Kew, London
PLA	Port of London Authority

Preface

The crucial importance of the Thames to London has been familiar to contemporaries and historians alike for centuries. For Fitz Stephen the Thames was 'that mighty river, teeming with fish' which enabled merchants 'from every nation that is under heaven' to carry their merchandise to London by ship.[1] In the reign of Henry VIII, it was reckoned to be, of all England's rivers, 'the moost commodious and profitable to all the Kinges liege people', contributing to the 'savegarde and ordering of the Kinges navy, conveyaunce of Marchauntdisses and other necessaries to and for the Kinges moost honorable Householde' and facilitating the activities of merchants trading into the surrounding hinterland as well as the city itself.[2] The central focus of contemporaries upon trade seems amply justified by surviving customs accounts, which show English commerce increasingly concentrated upon the Thames in the later middle ages until, by the 1540s, some three-quarters of measurable trade was channeled along the Thames axis between London and the emporia of the Low Coutries.[3]

The Thames was more than a commercial artery, however, no matter how vital. It was also a complex hydrological system, supporting a wide variety of ecosystems within and adjacent to the main channel of the river. The tidal nature of the river enhanced its value as a trade route, allowing larger vessels to penetrate up river, but human intervention had influenced the flow and the height of tides through embankment, reclamation, bridging and dredging. The natural resources of the river and the marshlands bordering the tidal Thames and its estuary – notably fisheries, wild fowl and reedbeds – were of value to Londoners, and were subject to repeated attempts at regulation, often at the cost of conflict with local Thames-side communities.[4] Fishing structures obstructed the flow of the channel and affected fish stocks and behaviour, while the reclamation of many marshes also changed the ecology of the river. The power of the tidal Thames and its tributaries was harnessed to operate mills, processing grain for metropolitan consumption, but that power could also be felt destructively, through storm

---

[1] W. Fitz Stephen, *Norman London* (New York, 1990), 49, 54.
[2] *Statutes of the Realm*, vol. 3 1509–1549 (1817), 550.
[3] C.M. Barron, *London in the Later Middle Ages* (Oxford, 2004), 90ff.
[4] Barron, *London*, 40–1.

flooding and tidal surges.[5] In all these areas the human and the natural interacted. The river was not a blank canvas upon which humans could draw. Every change made by human intervention provoked further changes in the river's hydrology and ecology, with profound implications for London and the other Thames-side communities. Industrial pollution and domestic effluent became crucial problems in the eighteenth and nineteenth centuries, but their impact upon the health of the river, and consequently upon human health, can be traced far back into the middle ages, when the disposal of night-soil and butchers' waste provoked controversy and repeated attempts at regulation.[6]

Despite much work on specific aspects of this human-natural interaction and mutual modification, there has as yet been no attempt at an integrated environmental history of the Thames. No equivalent of Marc Cioc's study of the post-1800 Rhine, or Nienhuis's multi-period survey of the Rhine-Meuse Delta yet exists.[7] Perhaps the nearest we have to a Thames environmental history is Alwyne Wheeler's marvellous study *The Tidal Thames*, published in 1979.[8] Wheeler was a zoologist and expert on fish biology, rather than a historian, but his book looks beyond the natural world and into the realm of human-natural interaction. The centre-piece of Wheeler's study was the restoration of the Thames between the 1950s and 1970s, when it was transformed from a grossly polluted, virtually lifeless waterway, into a substantially restored river with a rich returning fauna. However, Wheeler also examined the roots of the pollution crisis, through a survey of legislation and the writings of early naturalists, and attempted a history of individual fish species and their exploitation by the Thames fisheries. Also worthy of mention are Keene's pioneering exploration of the political, cultural and economic significance of water in medieval London, and of metropolitan regulation of this vital resource, and Ward's examination of the representation and 'reading' of the Thames during the climax of the Little Ice Age.[9] Taken together, these works point the way towards an integrated environmental history of the Thames which gives equal weight to natural processes, human interventions and the changing cultural meanings of the river.

The aims of the present small volume are more modest. It aspires to demonstrate some of the variety of work currently being undertaken on Thames history and archaeology, beyond the most common encapsulation of the Thames as a trade route. They arise from a conference on 'London, the Thames and Water'

---

[5] J.A. Galloway, 'Storm flooding, coastal defence and land use around the Thames estuary and tidal river, *c*.1250-1450', *Journal of Medieval History* 30 (2009), 1–18.

[6] E.L. Sabine, 'Butchering in mediaeval London', *Speculum* 8 (1933), 335–53.

[7] M. Cioc, *The Rhine: An Eco-Biography, 1815–2000* (Seattle, 2002); P.H. Nienhuis, *Environmental History of the Rhine-Meuse Delta* (New York, 2008).

[8] A. Wheeler, *The Tidal Thames: The History of a River and its Fishes* (London, 1979).

[9] D. Keene, 'Issues of water in medieval London', *Urban History* 21 (2008), 161–79; J.P. Ward, 'The taming of the Thames: reading the river in the seventeenth century', *Huntington Library Quarterly* 71 (2008), 55–75.

held at the Institute of Historical Research in October 2009.[10] Seven papers were presented there, of which five are published here.[11] Three of the papers (Galloway, Van Lieshout and Carlsson-Hyslop) explore the Thames as a hazard, as well as a resource, between the fourteenth and twentieth centuries. Freshwater flooding and North Sea storm surges were capable of wreaking considerable havoc along the Thames Estuary and tidal river, including the low lying parts of the metropolis. These three papers examine the impact of flooding, and the cultural, institutional and political response to the flood threat, at three different periods. Flooding emerges as an important influence upon the course of economic and environmental change in the later middle ages. The bodies which emerged to deal with floods and drainage became more formalised and stable over time, but the eighteenth-century city still had an essentially reactive set of institutions, dealing with problems at a local or micro-level. Such problems persisted into the twentieth century, when the storm surge of 1928 demonstrated the scale of the flood threat to large parts of central London. The funding of scientific research into the causes of storm surges and the development of city-wide flood defences required a transcending of old institutional structures and local mind-sets.

The remaining two papers are the work of archaeologists, a fitting reflection of the important work undertaken by teams based at the Museum of London and elsewhere on Thames-side sites over recent years and decades. Our understanding of the progressive extension of the Thames frontage, of London Bridge and of the shipping of the port of London, as well as of the river-side environment, have been transformed by the results of archaeological excavations since the 1970s and subsequent publication.[12] In this volume Goodburn and Davis present preliminary reports on two of the most exciting recent Thames-side finds, the tidal mills uncovered at Northfleet in NW Kent and at Greenwich. The former, dating from the late seventh century, and the latter from the 1190s constitute well-preserved examples of the mills which played a crucial role in the processing of grain for the medieval metropolis and the communities of the Thames Estuary. Such mills harnessed the power of the tidal river, but were also vulnerable to damage by extreme tides and storms. The ex-Templar mills in Southwark were described as 'broken and ruined by the inundation of the water of the Thames' in 1309,[13] and the Greenwich mill may also ultimately have succumbed to storms or rising river levels. Goodburn and Davis show that these mills have more to reveal than

[10] Organised as part of the Centre for Metropolitan History project 'London and the Tidal Thames 1250–1550: Marine Flooding, Embankment and Economic Change', for which see below.

[11] The other papers presented were Mike Berlin '"Large and strong houses": the impact of shipbuilding on the urban development of East London, circa 1580–1640' and Joe Hillier, 'Construction and conflict: unpacking constant water in 19th-century London'. Unfortunately, due to other commitments, Mike and Joe were unable to adapt their papers for publication in this volume.

[12] Much of this work is summarised in G. Milne, *The Port of Medieval London* (Stroud, 2003).

[13] Transcript of The National Archives: PRO E 368/79, fol. 111 dorse by H.J. Nicholson, online at <http://www.cf.ac.uk/hisar/people/hn/MilitaryOrders/MILORDOCS9.htm> accessed 15/6/2010.

the technology of milling, as they cast important light on the development of woodworking techniques and upon the medieval tidal regime. It is concluded that the Greenwich mill points to a significantly greater tidal range $c.1200$ than previously believed. To conclude the volume, Gustav Milne provides an overview of the work of the Thames Discovery Programme which, building on the work of the Thames Archaeological Survey, aims to encourage the widest possible participation in the surveying of the Thames foreshore, 'the longest archaeological site in the London region'. Sites ranging from prehistoric forests through medieval fish traps to the Blitz-damaged river walls of the mid twentieth century are being systematically recorded and fed into wider research agendas. This vital work is given added urgency by the knowledge that sites are constantly eroding, and that the river itself continually both reveals and destroys the evidence of its own history.

In preparing this volume for publication I would like to acknowledge the financial support of the Economic and Social Research Council, as part of the research project 'London and the Tidal Thames c.1250–1550: Marine Flooding, Embankment and Economic Change' (Award No. RES-000-22-2693). The Centre for Metropolitan History's Director, Matthew Davies, gave valuable advice and assistance. The participants in the one-day conference which gave rise to this volume provided many insights and comments, from which the contributors here have benefited; thanks are due to Derek Keene for coordinating discussion on that occasion. Particular thanks are due to Olwen Myhill, who played a major role in the organisation of the conference, and has also designed and typeset the volume.

James A. Galloway
Centre for Metropolitan History
Institute of Historical Research
School of Advanced Study
University of London

June 2010

List of contributors

ANNA CARLSSON-HYSLOP is a PhD student at the Centre for History of Science, Technology and Medicine at the University of Manchester

SIMON DAVIS is a Project Manager with Museum of London Archaeology

JAMES A. GALLOWAY was Researcher and Principal Investigator on the London and the Tidal Thames project at the Centre for Metropolitan History, Institute of Historical Research

DAMIAN GOODBURN is Woodwork Specialist at Museum of London Archaeology

GUSTAV MILNE is Project Director of the Thames Discovery Programme, hosted by the Thames Partnership and based at the Environment Institute, University College London

CARRY VAN LIESHOUT is a PhD student in the Department of Geography, King's College, University of London

1. Two new Thames tide mill finds of the 690s and 1190s and a brief up-date on archaeological evidence for changing medieval tidal levels*

DAMIAN GOODBURN WITH SIMON DAVIS

Aims of the paper

This paper aims to be a working interim statement on three related subjects on which archaeologists have been working recently in the greater London region and its estuarine borders. Specifically, it includes summary accounts of the initial results of the excavation of two previously unknown early tide mills, drawing together recently found archaeological evidence, from those two sites and others, to revise our understanding of medieval tidal conditions. In covering the contrasting mills of the 690s and 1190s several areas will be briefly touched on, including the situation of the mills, their degree of survival, their general layout, some key features of the woodworking technology embodied and, very cautiously, brief comments on their original working set up. In covering medieval river and estuary tidal levels it will be shown that we have had to revise our broadly accepted ideas about the tidal range of the Thames considerably, with some wider implications.

Introduction: systematic archaeological work on the banks of the Thames in the Greater London area

Building the foundations of a particular specialism for the Museum of London

Space only permits the briefest summary of how systematic archaeological investigations into the medieval Thames and it uses developed, but some key developments should be flagged up for readers new to the subject. The large scale redevelopment of the Thames frontages provided opportunities for Museum of London archaeologists to carry out rapid rescue excavations in the waterlogged areas where structures and finds were often very well preserved. These really got underway during the 1970s and by the mid 1980s G. Milne and others had been

* The authors would like to thank E. Biddulph and A. Hardy of Oxford Archaeology for making information and images available for this paper, and Union Railways Ltd who fund the work on the Ebbsfleet mill and Greenwich Wharf Ltd who funded the excavation of the Greenwich Mill site. We would also like to thank Dr J. Galloway and his team for organising the day conference at which this material was first discussed.

able to explore a number of themes and produce several publications still used for reference today on the changing construction of the mainly timber waterfront infra-structure, such as quay walls, jetties and docks, the layout of the port, evidence for tidal regimes and trading contacts shown by finds groups.[1] Archaeological evidence for the boats, ships and barges that worked in the medieval port was also gathered and published later by P. Marsden.[2] It must be understood that, although campaigns of excavation were also going on in other medieval port sites in Britain, virtually none have been extensively published. Waterfront archaeology is a special feature of London's archaeology. Tree-ring dating was applied to succeeding ranges of river frontages such that basic frameworks for dating important changes in woodworking technology started to be developed.

Timber, tree-rings and historic tidal levels in the 1970s and 80s

At that time no evidence for the harnessing of the tidal energy of the Thames had been found in the form of the remains of tide mills, though the location of several were suspected. However, G. Milne realised that tightly dated timber waterfront structures could be used to provide insights into medieval tidal regimes. This was done by linking, through careful stratigraphic recording, the date of the timber frontage to normally dry occupation levels adjacent to them thus producing pin points with which to plot expected high spring tide levels. The general view was developed that high spring tides were much lower than today reaching just under about +2m OD as opposed to +4.5m OD and more today. It was suggested that the tidal range was also much less, at *c.*3m on large spring tides[3] as opposed to around 7m today.

Further refining archaeological work in the waterfront zone up to the present day

From the end of the 1980s to the mid 1990s what had already become a comparatively methodological approach to archaeology along the Thames frontages was further refined in several ways. Several waterfront archaeologists began experimenting with medieval tools and materials to better understand medieval woodworking methods, which resulted in more targeted and accurate identification of key features such as distinctive tool marks and the use of different approaches to building in timber. Distinctions between later medieval timber frame 'carpentry' and other methods used earlier by Saxon and Norman period workers, became clearer.[4] Refinements in the taking of tree-ring samples also followed,

---

[1] G. Milne and C. Milne, *Medieval Waterfront Development at Trig Lane, London* (London and Middlesex Archaeological Society Special Paper No. 5, 1982).

[2] P. Marsden, *Ships of the Port of London Twelfth to Seventeenth Centuries AD* (English Heritage, Archaeological Report 5, 1996).

[3] Milne and Milne, *Trig Lane*, 60.

[4] D. Goodburn, 'Woods and woodland; carpenters and carpentry', in G. Milne (ed.), *Timber Building Techniques in London c. 900–1400* (London and Middlesex Archaeological Society Special Paper No. 15, 1992), 106–131.

resulting in extremely tight dating of timber structures and technological features. So by the late 1990s archaeological work had provided a vast archive of well recorded, closely dated material for waterfront archaeologists.

Another innovation led by G. Milne was the establishment of systematic attempts to survey and even excavate along the exposed Thames foreshore. This on-going campaign of work (for which see below) is extending what has been possible within the confines of development-led waterfront archaeology, and the fusion of data sets over the next few years will shed more light on the development of the medieval Thames, especially in areas such as the study of the tidal regime.

The horizontal double mill of 692 revealed at Northfleet during excavations ahead of the Channel Tunnel Rail Link

The circumstances of the Saxon mill find

The Channel Tunnel Rail Link project cut a swathe across the Kent countryside, aiming for a crossing point just west of Gravesend, running through the dammed off tidal inlet of the Ebbsfleet which joined the Thames at Northfleet. A team from Oxford Archaeology led by Richard Brown was commissioned to carry out excavations along the line of the route, which touched several known archaeological sites. The waterlogged remains of several phases of Roman creekside waterfront were found. The principal writer provided specialist assistance on-site concerning the woodwork found. Nearing the completion of the work in the area of the Roman timber waterfronts in 2002, another timber structure was found revetting the edge of a small island just to the east. The style of woodworking with thick cleft oak planking and half log piles suggested a probable Saxon date. Tree-ring spot dating by I. Tyers then confirmed that a date in the 690s was likely. The excavation team had by then revealed more of the structure, showing that the revetment was in fact a very well preserved mill dam surviving c.1.2m high and supporting the upper ends of two oak dugout chutes for a double mill. Ordnance Datum levels were taken on the top of the surviving mill dam, which can clearly be related to the expected high spring tides of the period (see below). It must be noted here that a detailed account of this structure and associated evidence is now very close to publication[5] and so only a brief outline based on the first-named writer's involvement with the project will be presented here.

The well preserved form of the mill is revealed

The remains of the mill were immediately recognised as of national importance and following the re-routing of the Ebbsfleet stream the excavation continued. This revealed the well preserved mill dam and pair of tapering dugout chutes for directing the stored tidal water onto the ladle-like arms of a pair of horizontal

---

[5] E. Biddulph and A. Hardy et al. in preparation, Oxford Archaeology monograph on Roman and Saxon Northfleet.

FIG. 1.1. The Ebbsfleet horizontal mill built in 692 AD, looking inland up the Ebbsfleet, showing the two hollowed chutes to the right, undercroft for two wheels centre and part of the tail race, left. Excavated by Oxford Archaeology.
(Photo: Oxford Archaeology)

FIG. 1.2. The Ebbsfleet horizontal mill built in 692 AD, looking down stream over the mill island showing the mill dam, left, and paired dugout chutes under excavation by the Oxford Archaeology field team.
(Photo: Oxford Archaeology)

wheels (Figs.1.1 and 1.2). Although the wheels had been removed in Saxon times fragments of two arms survived and the chutes with their upper sluice boards were largely intact. The surviving mill structure comprised several elements: the mill dam of thick cleft and hewn oak planks retained by cleft half log piles; the two rectangular section hollowed mill chutes; and a three-sided timber-lined undercroft in which the pair of wheels would have originally turned. In the simplest and most common form of this type of water mill to survive into the 'ethnographic present', the wheels turned in the horizontal plane with a direct drive shaft, extending up into the mill house, used to drive an adjustable upper millstone.

The undercroft was c.4m wide by c.2.7m in the direction of the water flow, with the chutes another 3.5m long. Beams forming the supports for parts of the mill machinery and its superstructure were also found inside the undercroft area. Immediately down stream the remains of a wattle-lined tail race was found. The floor of the undercroft was the only element not made of timber or wattle work, being of rammed Roman masonry from the adjacent villa complex. A short distance to the north a two phase, by-pass channel was found leading out of the largely wattle-lined, earth-banked mill pond. The by-pass channel was lined with dugout log chutes. One of the mill chutes appeared to have been bunged up, implying reduced running late in the life of the mill. Timbers left from the demolition of the structure were found lying in several phases of estuarine silt deposited during what must have been a period of fairly rapid sea level rise. This blanket of waterlogged silt led to the remarkable preservation found; in general this was a level of survival far in excess of that for the later Tamworth mill.[6]

Lifting the mill timbers for detailed examination and recording

The mill was recognised as of national importance due to its degree of preservation and early date. It was decided that the principal timbers ought to be lifted and hopefully conserved. This was done with the help of conservator D. Goodburn-Brown and her team. The timbers were then stored in water tanks in Chatham Historic Dockyard, where they were washed, recorded in detail and re-tanked by a multi-disciplinary team, organised by Oxford Archaeology, which comprised archaeologists and conservators; the primary author was seconded to lead the recording. Many features not recorded or seen under hurried and muddy site conditions were recorded, including traces of the use of very wide bladed broad axes to smooth the timbers after roughing out with narrow 'woodsmans' axes. Other features found included the use of yew for some of the fastenings where we might consider the use of metal today. But perhaps the most spectacular and strange finding was that of a faint but accurate, compass-drawn design on the roof of one of the chutes. This set of daisy wheels on daisy wheels was impossible to record photographically but was traced at 1:1 on film, as it seems to be the earliest

---

[6] P. Rhatz and R. Meeson, *An Anglo-Saxon Watermill at Tamworth* (Council for British Archaeology Research Report No.83, 1992).

engineering drawing in England. It appears to have been drawn to set out, at 1 to 1, the wheel hub slots for the arms on the water wheels.

Further tree-ring samples were taken and several fresh oak samples were dated by I. Tyers showing that the mill was built in 692 AD.

The mill of 692 AD sample of 'treewrightry' rather than carpentry

By contrast with the accuracy of the drawing we were also able to record all the classic features of pre-medieval approaches to structural woodwork in the way the woodwork of the mill had been done. These features include: no use of conventional mortice and tenon joints, or elaborate pre-fabrication methods requiring numbered joints; no use of saws; and the use of irregular cleft and hewn timbers and a range of simple axe-cut joints. No two matching timbers were the same. Many examples of this general approach to woodworking have been recorded up to and sometimes just after 1200 AD when the new 'carpentry' introduced in the 1180s starts to take over.[7] Accuracy only appears to have been used where essential in the Ebbsfleet mill machinery itself, whilst the rest of the woodwork resembles other excavated Saxo-Norman woodwork from southern England. The later mill construction echoes some of these early treewrightry approaches to building in timber, but also exhibits evidence of radically new techniques being introduced at the time.

The surprise find of a tide mill of 1194 at Greenwich

This discovery was of the remains of a massively built timber structure with unusual features transitional between treewrighting and carpentry.

In summer 2008 a small MoLA archaeological team were carrying out an archaeological watching brief on a large development site bordering the Thames in Greenwich.[8] Prehistoric wooden structures had been found in peat layers close by, but the key remains exposed were a large timber structure clearly of more recent date, with roughly rectangular beams up to 0.6 by 0.4m in section. The structure lay in the NE corner of the site, and continued under concrete foundations close to the main spoil heap for ground reduction. Unfortunately, safety conditions required that the excavation team, led by Senior Archaeologist A. Daykin, had to leave that part of the site for a week. The machine-exposed upper surfaces of the timbers were slightly dried out during that time but remained in fair condition. It was then that the complexity and importance of the find was recognised by Project Manager S. Davis, and the first named author was called in to provide advice on the interpretation of the timber remains, their recording and initial dating. Fortunately

---

[7] D. Goodburn, 'Timber studies', in J. Hill and A. Woodger (eds.), *Excavations at 72–75 Cheapside/ 83–93 Queen Street*, MoLAS Archaeological Studies 2 (1999).

[8] N. Faulkener with S. Davis, 'Water-power in medieval Greenwich', *Current Archaeology* 236 (2009), 30–35.

FIG. 1.3. The Greenwich tide mill built 1194 AD, showing the gridwork of massive oak
sill beams, looking west. Under excavation by MoLA.
(Photo: A. Chopping © MoLA)

the main foundation beam assembly of four crossing sills and two larger beams
running approximately N–S (Fig. 1.3) had many joints cut into them and surface
finishes and tool marks surviving. These features were used to suggest a rough
date bracket by analogy with the dated corpus of such features from the London
region and elsewhere. A dating in the later twelfth century was suggested, as
although there were typical early 'carpentry' notched lap joints used for removed

7

braces, other features such as the way some of the large sill beams were made by controlled cleaving and hewing a pair from the parent log, were more typical of treewrighting.[9] That is, the structure exhibited features of both approaches to building in timber. Other examples include the use of a mix of mortice-like joints from mortices for posts very similar to later medieval examples alongside through-sockets for tusk tenons and tapered socket joints for joist ends which are found in treewrighting, but not typical English timber frame carpentry.

The large structure is recognised as a mill

At first the possibility that the grid of very low lying beams was the base of a robust timber tower was considered, but closer examination showed that the central area of the gridwork of beams had originally been floored over and was rather water worn. Also the structure was set extremely low in relation to the approximate levels which large spring tides would have reached based on findings from other London sites of the *c.* twelfth-century period such as at Billingsgate and Bull Wharf, where normally dry surfaces were found at just under +2.0m OD.[10] The upper face of the gridwork of sill beams lay at around –0.5m OD; they would have been permanently wet in that period. By the end of the visit it was clear that a tidemill had been found of around the later twelfth century. The recent foundations that were partly covering the structure were carefully removed and a complex assembly of timbers exposed by hand excavation. To our surprise a great deal of medieval woodwork survived including the delicate remains of part of a vertically-set mill wheel with some of its paddle and spoke fittings intact (Fig. 1.4). The section of oak wheel rim was just under one-fifth of the wheel rim and initial calculations show that it may have been just over 5m in diameter. The wheel had turned in a large dugout trough that was much patched and for a while looked as if it may have been a reused dugout boat! However, as the excavation progressed it became clear that the oak trough just formed the base of a deep narrow plank-lined channel which had been largely dismantled. The base of the trough in which the wheel turned was at –1.15m OD, a very significant low level discussed below. To the north side of the trough lay an arrangement of small oak beams used to support what appears to have been two phases of floor planking. This plank-lined area must have once accommodated the gearing wheels necessary to turn the energy of the horizontal wheel shaft so that it would drive a vertical shaft.

Foundations for what must have been a substantial mill house above the wheel level were necessarily large in the saturated ground; most of the timbers lay on a layer of rammed chalk cobbles and were further supported by massive squared

[9] Goodburn, 'Timber studies'.
[10] G. Milne, *The Port of Medieval London* (Stroud, 2003), 144–46 succinctly states the general understanding of relative tidal levels of the inner estuary of the Thames in the medieval period known then, though unpublished evidence from Bull Wharf suggests the shore side occupation level would have been a little over +2m OD.

Fig. 1.4. The Greenwich tide mill built 1194 AD, looking east (inland),
showing the gridwork of sill beams, lighter joisted floor in the foreground and long
narrow dugout base to the wheel pit with a section of wheel under excavation by MoLA.
(Photo: D. Goodburn)

oak piles with tusk tenoned cross bars forming a sort of cradle. Additionally the
central N–S sill beam was supported on a line of close set log piles, mainly of
oak, and the landward side of this foundation was sheathed with cleft oak boards
set on end and linked with tongue and groove joints. These slightly irregular, but
very strong boards, had been trial fitted on land first and numbered so they could
be quickly fitted and pegged into a rebate in the sill beam during the very short
tidal window available. At the lowest levels on the riverward side of the mill, four
short lengths of oak sill beam were found set on top of pairs of piles with tusk
tenoned heads. These short sills also supported four main squared oak uprights
that must have supported the riverward side of the mill house. Despite the massive
and intricate foundations used there was clearly some subsidence during the life
of the mill and it may have been a factor in its eventual abandonment and partial
demolition. Again a rapid ingress of estuarine clay silt helped to preserve the
timbers of the site and the site became forgotten seemingly leaving no trace in
local placenames, although a small relict inlet area is sometimes shown on some of
the maps. Initial historical research shows that the mill lay on land belonging to St
Peter's Abbey at Ghent. Tree-ring dating by I. Tyers, of the large gridwork of sill
beams shows that the mill was built in 1194 and in due course more documentary
information is likely to be found after the current period of stasis before the tail
race area of the mill can be investigated, hopefully later this year (2010).

Finally, during that phase of excavation it was decided that several key elements of the mill should be lifted and preserved for display alongside graphics and possibly models showing what the mill as a whole looked like.

Mysterious features of the Greenwich tide mill and further work

Clearly such a large complex structure as the remains of this tide mill will require considerable further study once the last phase of excavation is complete. This will be a multi-disciplinary effort involving internal MoLA specialists in early woodworking, geoarchaeology, palaeobotany, the excavation team and external specialists such as historical hydromechanical engineer Dr Robert Spain, who has already kindly produced a preliminary reconstruction drawing of the waterwheel and offered some initial ideas to explain the curious layout of parts of the mill as found. He has suggested that the central part of the gridwork of sill beams that was clearly close boarded as a large lined water channel to prevent erosion, may in fact have been an earlier, larger wheel pit. This may make considerable sense as the offset location and small size of the wheel found may possibly suggest it was the last stage in the use of a slowly collapsing mill. This and other queries will be followed up during the post excavation study in due course. Perhaps the strangest feature of the site is the lack of a clear tidal holding pond or network of channels feeding the landward side of the mill. However, the second named author has discovered historical evidence of peat digging in the vicinity and that may have removed clear traces of embankments and a head race, normally robust indicators of an early mill site.

New archaeological evidence for medieval tidal levels on the Thames: an overview

Terminology

It is crucial that researchers state what type of tidal level they are seeking to reconstruct for the past as great confusion may otherwise arise. The highest astronomically predicted tide (HAT), which is reached only a few times a year, is sometimes cited as the level where shore side residents would have built their floors, roads and hearths down to. But in the first named author's modern experience of living over 25 years besides tidal waters in south-east England this was not generally the case except for large modern developments built with an eye open to sea level rise as a result of global warming. Traditionally shore side dwellers and workers in the south-east have built quays, jetties, etc to levels somewhere between HAT and mean high water spring tides. A small amount of minor flooding was put up with, or dealt with by the use of simple low barriers such as doorstep flood boards. The advantages of being very close to the waterfront outweighed a certain dampness and occasional more serious flooding with exceptional surge tides. This sort of situation can be seen in the archaeological record as well along the historic Thames as fine silt and sand layers over normally dry shore side

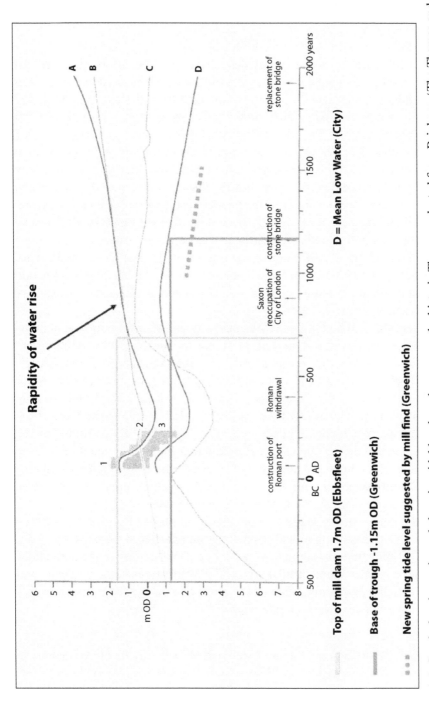

Fig. 1.5. Graph showing estimated changing tidal levels and ranges on the historic Thames, adapted from Brigham, 'The Thames and Southwark waterfront', with new tidal level points derived from the top of the Ebbsfleet mill dam of 692 AD and the base of the wheel pit of the 1194 Greenwich mill shown as bold corners above the respective dates. The bold dashed line indicates a conservative estimated minimum drop in low neap tide levels necessary to allow the mill wheel to turn. During large spring tides the low tide level must have been appreciably lower, to at least −3.5m OD.

11

surfaces such as quay sides and lanes. So this slightly blurred but pragmatic level is what needs to be kept in mind here.

Filling in gaps in the early medieval data

These two mill excavations have provided very useful new information on tidal ranges for their periods which are helping to deepen our understanding of later medieval tidal regimes and fill in gaps in the data from the late Roman period to the ninth century AD. The height on the top of the surviving mill dam of 692 AD at Ebbsfleet was *c.*+1.7m OD, showing that there had been a rapid rise in the area from around 300 AD when occupation levels nearby were recorded at *c.*0 OD.[11] More sites from this period are needed to act as a check on the data and particularly to try to define just how fast the known late to post-Roman rise in relative sea levels actually was. Development along the Thames estuary is starting to provide these sites which will hopefully be carefully investigated to find datable timber structures and associated hearths and occupation surfaces. Currently it would appear that the rise in high spring tide levels from middle Saxon times (represented by the Ebbsfleet mill dam best of all) until the late medieval period is clear but moderate, reaching *c.*2.75m OD in London at the head of the estuary by the fifteenth century.[12]

The later tidal mill find at Greenwich has provided no information about how high the larger spring tides of the year 1194 rose to, but has shed very important light on the likely low tide levels and thereby the tidal range or 'amplitude'. For the wheel of a tide mill to work effectively it must be clear of tidal water on the downward side for a considerable period, at least a third and possibly half the tidal range. So an OD level as low as −1.15m OD at the base of the wheel, allowing for compaction, say, just over −1.0m OD, about 3m below the top of the normal spring tide range, suggests that the range would have been much greater. How much greater is clearly a guesstimate on which we will take extensive moulinological advice once the field project is finished, but a drop of 1.5–2.5m depending on the type of tide, would seem likely. Thus, the tidal range in the inner estuary leading to the medieval port of London can be seen to have been far greater than had been suggested earlier at perhaps 4.5–5.5m instead of around 3m on spring tides (see above). This greater range in the tides also implies a greater speed of tidal flow which would have helped trade up and down the estuary, providing much of the motive force needed to move barges and shipping even against moderate winds.

---

[11] T. Brigham, 'The Thames and Southwark waterfront in the Roman Period', in B.Watson, T. Brigham, and T. Dyson, *London Bridge 2000 years of a River Crossing* (MoLAS Monograph 8, 2001), 12–27.

[12] S. Blatherwick and R. Bluer, *Great Houses, Moats and Mills on the South Bank of the Thames: Medieval and Tudor Southwark and Rotherhithe* (Museum of London Archaeology Monograph 47, 2009), 57.

Although findings from new shore-side excavations have prompted this reappraisal of tidal ranges, some earlier excavation results and synthesis have quite strongly hinted at a much greater tidal range than *c*.3m. The iron work on the stern post of the Blackfriars III barge or 'shout'[13] which sank in the early fifteenth century clearly shows that she had a stern rudder which had been removed, as had much of her other salvageable equipment. This suggests to the first named writer that there was probably access on low spring tides to where she lay, between –2 to –3m OD near the mouth of the River Fleet. This would have required a tidal range of around 5m at that time. Other suggestive evidence has been collated by G. Milne who cited the height of at least one wharf front at the Tower to be 5m high.[14] Clearly this would fit a tidal range somewhere near 5m rather than one of only 3m.

In sum

It is hoped that this brief statement of work in progress has further demonstrated the ability of systematic archaeology along the frontages of the Thames and its tributaries to provide information of local, regional, national or even international value in many fields. The fields covered here of changing woodworking technology, the development of mills and early engineering and evidence for relative sea-level change are central themes, but other important topics relating to the Thames include navigation, trade, ship and boat building, waterside industries, fishing and subsistence. The Thames provided a great many positive functions for London and its large hinterland, but was also the source of disasters such as flooding, which are discussed in other papers in this volume.

---

[13] Marsden, *Ships*, 64.
[14] Milne and Milne, *Trig Lane*, 60.

2.   'Piteous and grievous sights': the Thames marshes at the close of the middle ages

JAMES A. GALLOWAY

In the late 1520s Thomas Cromwell, soon to become Henry VIII's chief minister and vicar-general, was legal secretary to Cardinal Wolsey, and much occupied with the affairs of the Cardinal's new colleges in Oxford and Ipswich. A total of 30 mainly small religious houses had been dissolved and their lands appropriated in support of the colleges, work on which began in 1525. Among these was Lesnes in Kent, an abbey of Augustinian Canons located on the edge of the extensive tract of Thames marshes between Woolwich and Erith (Fig. 2.1).

The Lesnes possessions, which were surrendered in February 1525, were concentrated near the river, including the manors of Lesnes, and Fulhams in neighbouring Plumstead.[1] Here were extensive embanked marshlands, protected from the river and the tides since at least the early thirteenth century, and held as a combination of demesne and holdings leased out to numerous tenants. These lands were used as high-yielding arable land and pasture, and had in the past proved profitable, especially given the proximity of the London market. Fisheries in the Thames and the marshes were also valuable assets, and the 'poor lieges of Lesnes, Plumstead, Erith, Woolwich and Greenwich' had petitioned the King in the 1390s to be allowed to continue fishing with boats, nets and 'engines' (weirs or kiddles) and thereby supplying 'all the surrounding countryside' as well as the City of London.[2]

The aim of Wolsey's expropriation was clearly to sell off profitable lands and goods as quickly as possible, in order to raise money for the Cardinal's building works. At Lesnes, however, things went wrong from the start. A William Harrys, who appears to have been in day-to-day charge of affairs at Lesnes, wrote to Cromwell at some point in 1526 informing him of a 'brekk' or breach, that had damaged the river walls and drainage ditches. 'I was never so troubled in my life', wrote Harrys, who had had to promise the labourers repairing the damage payment out of his own purse.[3] The breach seems to have been patched up, and

---

[1] E. Hasted, *The History and Topographical Survey of the County of Kent: Volume 2* (1797), 203–63.

[2] The National Archives (TNA), PRO SC/8/22/1061.

[3] *Letters and Papers, Foreign and Domestic, of the Reign of Henry VIII* (hereafter *L&P Hen VIII*), 21 vols. (London, 1864–1920), vol. 4 pt. 2, *1526–8*, 1231.

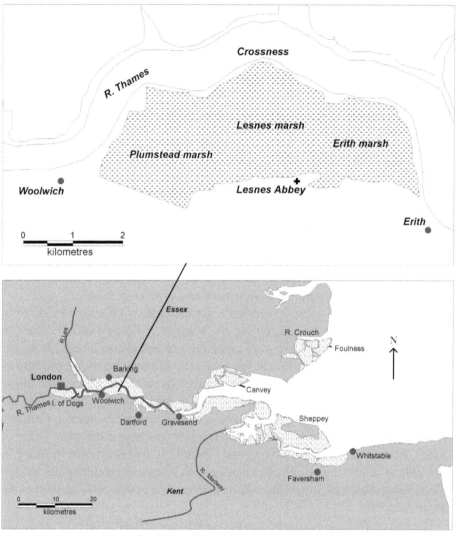

FIG. 2.1. The marshlands bordering the tidal river Thames and Thames Estuary, with detail of Lesnes, Erith and Plumstead marshes.

surveyors were sent to measure and value the lands at Lesnes, where there were supposed to be 600 acres of marsh.[4] However, before any sale of the Lesnes lands could be effected a further and more calamitous flood ensued. In January 1529 Cromwell wrote to Stephen Gardiner, Wolsey's chief secretary, that he had visited the scene:

> *I have been at Lysenes where I saw one of the most pyteous and greuous sightes that ever I saw – which to me before the Sight of the same was incredyble – concernyng*

---

[4] *L&P Hen VIII, vol. 4 pt. 2, 1526–8, 2245.*

the breche out of the Thames into the marshes at Lyesnes, which be all ouerflowen and drowned. And that at the last chaunge the tyde was so high that there happened a new breche which hathe fordone as moche worke there as will cost £300 [in]... new making of the same...[5]

If money was not immediately forthcoming, Cromwell continued, great hurt would be done to the country and to the 'King's stream' [the Thames] in addition to the total loss of the ground and lands belonging to the college there.

The cause of these particular incidents of flooding seems likely to have been institutional. The abbey's functions as landowner had been taken over by Wolsey's agents, and with them the responsibility to maintain river defences, in cooperation with neighbouring landlords and tenants, and to contribute to general levies ordered by the Commissioners of Sewers for marsh defence work. As the prime reason for acquiring the abbey's lands was to sell them as quickly as possible, it seems likely that these maintenance works were not regarded as a high priority, and local expertise and advise may have been disregarded. Certainly there is evidence in Harris and Cromwell's letters of resentment and lack of cooperation. Harris relates how he would rather have begged for his bread than continued at Lesnes 'in pain and cold and watching, with hatred of poor men and laborers'. Another of the Cardinal's men, Stephen Vaughan, complained to Cromwell of lack of cooperation in surveying the abbey's lands: 'People here are so obstinate', he wrote, complaining that it took four days to find someone who would show him the marshlands in Plumstead belonging to the manor of Fulhams.[6]

However, the flooding at Lesnes falls into a wider picture of decay and deterioration along the Thames at the close of the middle ages, which cannot solely be attributed to institutional factors, but which appear to have underlying economic and environmental causes. The breaches that Cromwell observed were neither the first nor the last to affect the marshes in what would later be known as the Woolwich and Erith Level. The years of social and economic disruption following the Black Death had seen widespread flooding around the Thames, and the marshes at Plumstead, Erith and Lesnes were the subject of several commissions *de walliis et fossatis* at that period.[7] The Abbot of Lesnes had received a commission in November 1373, at another period of widespread flooding.[8] A century later his successor, together with the Abbot of St Augustine's

---

[5] R.B. Merriman, *Life and Letters of Thomas Cromwell*, vol I: *Life, Letters to 1535* (Oxford, 1902), 324–5.

[6] *L&P Hen VIII*, vol 4. pt. 2, *1526–8*, 2245

[7] *Calendar of Patent Rolls* (hereafter, *CPR*) (London, 1892 onwards). The issuing of commissions *de walliis et fossatis* was the standard royal response to problems of flooding and drainage. Commissions were issued to local landholders and others, giving power to enforce cooperation among neighbours so that necessary works and repairs were carried out. See J.A. Galloway, 'Storm flooding, coastal defence and land use around the Thames estuary and tidal river, *c*.1250–1450', *Journal of Medieval History* 30 (2009). 1–18, at p. 8.

[8] *CPR 1370–4*, 314.

Canterbury, the lords of neighbouring Plumstead, were among the recipients of a commission issued in 1474 for the 'coast and... marsh' between the towns of Woolwich and Northfleet.[9]

By the early sixteenth century, therefore, the marshes at Lesnes and adjacent areas had a considerable history of embankment and flooding, and institutions existed to cope with the repeated environmental challenges. The tenants of Lesnes Abbey were obliged to make regular payments for maintenance of the marsh defences, at a rate of 4d per acre according to a surviving roll from 1462–3.[10] These marshes were expensive to defend against the tides, however. Manorial accounts for the possessions of the Queen in Erith marsh indicate a fluctuating, but generally high level of expenditure on repairs to river walls and marsh ditches in the years around 1500 (Fig. 2.2). In the years 1510–15 expenditure never falls below £10 per year, and in 1512–13 reached £15. After 1515, although the series of accounts for the Queen's other manors, including Swanscombe, continues, the record of repairs carried out at Erith just stops. That this was caused by something more than merely a change in accounting procedure is strongly suggested by an entry from nearly twenty years later, in the account for 1533–4.[11] The accountant explains that an 80% reduction in the amount of the farm – the annual rent paid for the Queen's 218 marshland acres – was to be applied, 'because the said lands have for a long time past been submerged by a great flow [*magn'flux*'] of sea-water'. This sounds very like a storm surge – one of those intense displacements of sea-water driven by the movement of deep low pressure systems into the southern North Sea basin, which can raise water levels several metres above normal high tides.[12]

On 26 December 1516 – the year following the last account of repairs to the marsh defences at Erith – a damaging surge is recorded on the other side of the North Sea, affecting Zeeland and Flanders.[13] Furthermore, there is definite evidence to show that this storm surge affected the tidal Thames, and specifically impacted upon the Erith area. A book of payments made by the controller of the English King's ships refers to a 'great and high tide that was upon St Stephen's Day [26 Dec] 1516', which wet ropes and cables in the storehouse at Erith. In response, expenditure was authorised on raising the doors of the storehouse 'for keeping out of the high tides'.[14] Putting all these references together it seems reasonable to infer that the initial flooding of Erith marshes was caused by this same storm

---

[9] *CPR 1467–77*, 463.

[10] *L&P Hen VIII*, vol. 4 pt. 2, *1526–8*, 1593.

[11] TNA, PRO SC6/Hen VIII/6552

[12] A. McRobie, T. Spencer and H. Gerritsen, 'The Big Flood: North Sea Storm Surge', *Philosophical Transactions of the Royal Society*, Series A, vol. 363, no. 1831 (2005), 1263–70. See also Anna Carlsson-Hyslop's paper in this volume.

[13] E. Gottschalk, *Stormvloeden en Rivieroverstromingen in Nederland*, 3 vols. (Assen, 1971–78), vol. 3 appendix XI.

[14] *L&P Hen VIII* vol. 2 pt. 2, *1517–18*, 1406.

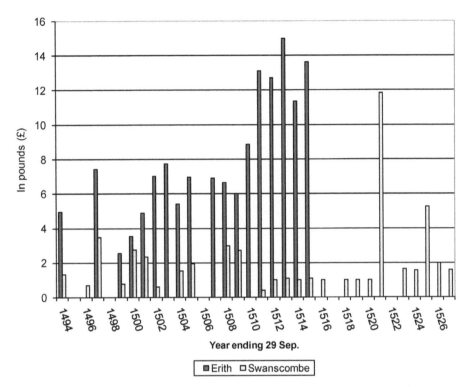

FIG. 2.2. Expenditure on maintenance of river walls and marsh drainage on the manors of Erith and Swanscombe, 1494–1527.
(Source: The National Archives, PRO SC6/HenVII/1423–47, HenVIII/6530–47)

surge, and that the damage was sufficiently severe to lead to the abandonment of attempts to maintain the river-walls for an extended period, leaving the Queen's demesne acres subject to the tides.

The flooding at Lesnes in the 1520s, which seems to owe much to institutional disruption, thus added to an already deteriorating situation in the marshes between Woolwich and Erith. Worse was to follow. A further powerful storm surge is known to have occurred in November 1530, causing devastation in the Low Countries. In Flanders and Zeeland large areas of land were lost in the 'St Felix's flood' and there was considerable loss of life.[15] The surge also hit the Thames Estuary and tidal river, albeit with less deadly consequences. The chronicler Holinshed wrote that on the 4th and 5th of November 'was a great wind that blew down many houses and trees, after which wind followed so high a tide that it drowned the marshes on Essex side and Kent, with the Isle of Thanet and other places, destroying much cattle'. This must have exacerbated an already serious situation in the Erith and neighbouring marshes. An 'Acte Concerning Plumsted Marsh' was passed by Parliament two months later, in January 1531, which in its preamble

[15] P.H. Nienhuis, *Environmental History of the Rhine-Meuse Delta* (New York, 2008), 247–8.

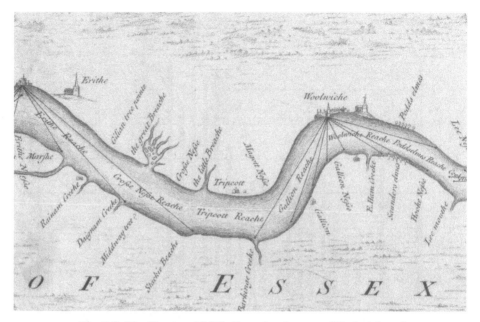

Fig. 2.3. The Great and Little Breaches between Woolwich and
Erith in 1588. Note: this map was drawn with north at the bottom.
(Detail from British Library Maps, Crace XVIII no. 17, reproduced with permission)

refers to 'the outrageousness' of the river Thames having drowned the marshes of Plumsted and Lesnes through breaches in the marsh walls of Plumstead, Lesnes and Erith. Repair work was being undertaken on the Plumstead breach, and a new cross-wall constructed, running from the Thames to the uplands, to prevent the penetration of the flood-waters which were entering the level at the more serious Erith breach.[16]

A map drawn in 1588 depicts two breaches between Woolwich and Erith, 'the great breach' and 'the lesser breach' (Fig. 2.3). The Great Breach, which was still not repaired by the date of this map, is almost certainly the one referred to in 1531. This map has north at the bottom, so the great breach lay to the east of Crossness, between the Ness and what is marked as Gilian Tree point and is today known as Jenningtree Point. When it was eventually repaired in the seventeenth century, a characteristic set-back or horse-shoe wall was constructed around the scoured out hole where the tidal waters had passed in and out through the breach, visible on the first edition Ordnance Survey map.

The 1531 Act sought to enforce the payment of cess, scot and other charges levied with the authority of the Commissioners of Sewers, in order to fund the continuing attempts to recover and protect the lands which had been flooded. In this, it appears to have failed almost entirely. 'The Kings works at Lesnes are

[16] *Statutes of the Realm,* vol. 3 (1817), 320.

much hindered because the cesses are unpaid', Cromwell was advised in 1533.[17] Following Wolsey's fall the Lesnes lands were in royal hands, and the King, 'our great owner there', was amongst those in arrears, for 420 acres of marshland. Sir Edward Boughton wrote in July 1533 that the workmen had been unpaid for six weeks, and that he '[could not] get a penny of £250 owing by divers owners', among others by the monastery of Westminster.[18] 'It is time to know what should be done about the measurement of the lands at Lesenes', Boughton continued, 'or else the ditches cannot be made in convenient time to drain them, and without them the marshes cannot be sown or pastured'. Meanwhile, the Abbot of St Augustine's, Canterbury, the biggest land-holder in Plumstead marsh wrote to Cromwell in 1535, thanking him (perhaps through metaphorically clenched teeth) for his kindness to the House and explaining that 'the marsh of Plumsted [had] so impoverished him of money and jewels that he [could not] recompense Cromwell's goodness except by prayer.'[19]

The efforts made consequent upon the 1531 Act to enforce payment of cesses and other local taxes, and to coordinate operations in the marshes, seem ultimately to have been ineffective. Despite the commitment of substantial sums by the Crown and other landholders a petition to Parliament, early in the reign of Elizabeth I, narrated how 2,000 acres in Erith, Plumstead and Lesnes, which had in former times 'comprised good pasture grounds and meadows', had during the previous 30 years been 'laid waste by breaches and inundations of the Thames'.[20] This suggests that most of the marshland peninsula between Woolwich and Erith was still at this date (1561) unreclaimed, and subject to the tides. Efforts continued, sporadically, to definitively close the breaches and reclaim the flooded lands. Conflicts of interest arose, however, as the marshes in their flooded state provided a livelihood for fishermen and others who could harvest the wild or semi-wild resources of saltmarsh, creeks and mudflats. In 1577 we hear that fishermen from Barking, Picardy and other places were greatly hindering work to repair the Great Breach at Erith 'by passing to and fro with their boats over the same'. The fishermen were to be barred from approaching within ten roods of the breach under pain of punishment.[21] The struggle to recover and keep these marshes free from tidal influence continued for many decades thereafter, as the 1588 map bears testimony, and the breaches were not to be finally and definitively repaired until well into the seventeenth century.[22]

Here, we can see, the reclamation work of the sixteenth and seventeenth centuries was not pioneer work, embanking and bringing into intensive cultivation

---

[17] *L&P Hen VIII*, vol. 6, *1533*, 373.

[18] *L&P Hen VIII*, vol. 6, *1533*, 386.

[19] *L&P Hen VIII*, vol. 7, *1534*, 567.

[20] W. Dugdale, *The History of Imbanking and Draining* (2nd edn., London, 1777), 63.

[21] *Acts of the Privy Council of England*, New Series vol. X, *1577–8*, ed. J.R. Dasent (London, 1895), 23.

[22] Dugdale, *Imbanking*, 65.

lands which had always previously been tidal saltmarsh or mudflat, but rather represented the recovery of lands which had already had a long history of embankment and drainage. Early fourteenth-century documentation for Erith shows the marshes there in use as intensive arable farmland as well as meadow and pasture. Two hundred and fourty-four acres of marsh arable belonged to the holding of Giles de Badlesmere in 1338, and were valued at 36d per acre, as high as any land in England at this date, and six times higher per acre than arable on the neighbouring uplands – a striking reflection of the fertility of the alluvial marsh soils. Lesnes Abbey's demesne farms provided the abbey with significant profits, as shown by surviving fourteenth-century obedientaries accounts.[23] In the 1360s sales of grain and legumes had brought in over £30 per year, much of it from beans – an important marshland crop – sold in London and Dartford. Other major sources of income included sales of wool and livestock, while reeds growing beside the Thames wall were harvested and sold in the capital. Edward Boughton's comments, cited above, show that the land-use in the sixteenth century Lesnes marshes, once secured and drained, was expected to include both arable and pasture land.

This sixteenth-century recovery of marshlands previously embanked, but now regularly covered by the tides, can be seen at a range of other locations around the Thames. Close to London, Wapping marsh was recovered in the 1540s by the Fleming Cornelius Wanderdelf, after being, in the words of an Act of Parliament, 'longe tyme surrounded and over flowen with water.'[24] The Isle of Dogs, which had supported a small community of mixed farmers in the fourteenth and early fifteenth centuries, was flooded in 1448 when the river wall opposite Deptford was breached.[25] The settlement of marsh and the chapel belonging to Pomfret manor were abandoned, and the isle lay subject to high tides for the next four decades. In the 1460s the Bishop of London was receiving 40s per year from fishing and fowling in the marsh, together with a half-share of the reeds cut there. The marsh was recovered in 1488 on the initiative of the then Bishop Thomas Kempe, but then at least partially flooded again; in 1524 482 ½ acres were described as having been recovered for a second time by William Morowe of Stepney and others.[26] Some parts were evidently still flooded in 1529.[27]

The marshes of East Ham, North Woolwich and the West Marsh of Barking were in the process of piece-meal recovery in the early sixteenth century, after well over a century of inundation which had begun with the breaching of river-walls by two or more powerful storm surges in the 1370s. The lands of the Abbess of Barking

[23] TNA, PRO SC6/1108/7 and 8.

[24] *Statutes of the Realm*, vol. 3, 966.

[25] *A History of the County of Middlesex* (Victoria County History) vol. 11, ed. T.F.T. Baker (London, 1998), 1–7, 52–63.

[26] *L&P Hen VIII,* vol. 4 pt. 1, *1524–6*, 230.

[27] *L&P Hen VIII,* vol. 4 pt. 3 *1529–30*, 2366.

and the Abbot of Stratford were amongst those flooded, and within a decade a pragmatic adaptation to the changing environment is evident, with exploitation shifting from demesne farming and leasing to tenant farmers to the licensing of fishing weirs or kiddles placed in the flooded marshes.[28] The Abbesses of Barking appealed – often successfully – for relief from taxes and other obligations on account of the loss of their lands and income, not just in the immediate aftermath of the 1370s floods, but for a century and more thereafter. Thus, in 1462 a grant was made to the Abbess and Convent of return of writs, and of fines, forfeitures and other perquisites within the hundred of Becontree, 'on account of the losses that they have sustained by a great part of their land being inundated by the river Thames.'[29] Some of the marshes in East and West Ham were recovered on the initiative of William Hicheman, Abbot of Stratford between 1499 and 1516.[30] Barking Abbey was also proceeding to reclaim its flooded marshes in the early sixteenth century, and at the time of the house's dissolution in 1539 various parcels of marsh were described as 'lately recovered'.[31]

At other locations along the tidal river, retrenchment may have been more typical than the abandonment of large areas of marsh. At Wennington and Aveley, to the east of Barking and Dagenham, an indenture was drawn up in February 1500 between John Barret of Aveley, gentleman and Richard Jones, a labourer from Lambeth, whereby Jones was to 'in' 42 acres of marshland for a payment of 40 marks.[32] These acres may possibly have been part of the 'lands and meadows' flooded in Aveley, Rainham and Wennington 'by a sudden flood of the Thames' in or before 1452, and for which the inhabitants of those parishes had appealed for a remission of their contributions to a tenth and fifteenth.[33]

Further out into the estuary, schemes were in hand by the 1530s to embank the extensive marshlands of the Hoo peninsula. Documentary and archaeological evidence indicates that the marshes here were at least partly embanked and drained by the fourteenth century, notably in holdings of the Priory of Christ Church, Canterbury.[34] It is striking, then, to find in a map drawn of the marshes in the 1530s that virtually all are described as salt marsh, rather than 'inned' marsh.[35] Only at Cooling is inned marsh depicted on this map, and the legend

---

[28] J.A. Galloway and J. Potts, 'Marine flooding in the Thames estuary and tidal river c.1250–1450: impact and response', *Area* 39 (2007), 370–9, at pp. 374–5.

[29] *CPR 1461–7*, 223

[30] *A History of the County of Essex* (Victoria County History), vol. 6, ed. W.R.Powell (London, 1973), 14–18.

[31] W.M. Sturman,'Barking abbey: a study in its external and internal administration from the conquest to the dissolution', PhD. thesis, University of London (1961), 75.

[32] Essex Record Office, D/DL/T1/566.

[33] *CPR 1452–61*, 57.

[34] E.E.M. Bowler, 'The reclamation and land-use of the Thames marshes of North West Kent', Ph.D. thesis, University of London (1968), 157ff.

[35] BL Harley Ms 590 f.1, viewable online at <http://www.bl.uk/onlinegallery/onlineex/unvbrit/v/zoomify82953.html> (accessed 29/5/2010).

explains that this work had been undertaken by then current Lord Cobham, who owned the principal manor there. Around the mouth of the Medway too, many marshes which had in the thirteenth and fourteenth centuries been embanked and cultivated were by the sixteenth century again part of the inter-tidal zone. Sharpness and Slayhills marshes had been devastated by storm surges in the early fifteenth century, and their rental and tithe value had collapsed.[36] Lands alienated in mortmain to Faversham Abbey in 1506 included marshland and sheep pasture in Luddenham, 'now submerged by inundation of salt water'.[37]

Why had so many marshes around the Thames apparently reverted to tidal salt-marsh at the close of the middle ages? One possible explanation is that the later middle ages saw an increase in storminess compared to earlier and later centuries, and that the flooding was thus a direct result of this increasing natural hazard, augmented by a gradual rise in relative sea-level. Some evidence from the Low Countries seems to suggest that this happened. Major floods described by chroniclers, which in their intensity and widespread effects, can be identified as storm surges, appear to become progressively more frequent between the twelfth and the sixteenth centuries, before declining again thereafter. This emerges from the encyclopaedic work of Elizabeth Gottschalk.[38] Other types of evidence are more equivocal. Expenditure on the repair of dykes and harbours points to periods of intense storm activity – such as the first quarter of the fifteenth century – without a clear long-term trend.[39] The available evidence from the Thames Estuary is not yet good enough to make a definitive judgement, but at the moment tends to support the latter picture.

Contemporaries appear to have been aware that lands which had once been dry farmland were now subject to tidal flooding, and they were inclined to blame an increasingly violent and unpredictable nature. This emerges from a fascinating petition presented to the Crown by the Parliament of 1489, evidently at the instigation of the London authorities, concerning the Conservancy (the oversight or jurisdiction) of the River Thames:

> *The commons assembled in this present parliament pray your highness, that where the mayor of your city of London at the time is a conservator having the conservation of the water and river Thames from the bridge of Staines to the waters of Yantlet and Medway, it is the case that within a few years, due to storms and the great abundance of water in the said river Thames, various breaches, overflows and creeks have appeared and grown out of the said river Thames, and drowned and flooded various pastures, meadows and grounds of various persons, in which breaches, overflows, creeks and flooded ground the fish fry and spawn mostly*

---

[36] Galloway and Potts, 'Marine flooding', 374.
[37] *CPR 1494–1509*, 497.
[38] Gottschalk, *Stormvloeden*.
[39] A.M.J. de Kraker, 'Reconstruction of storm frequency in the North Sea area of the preindustrial period, 1400–1625 and the connection with reconstructed time series of temperatures', *History of Meteorology* 2 (2005), 51–70.

remain, and in the same places the said fry and spawn are taken daily in great number by the fishermen there, with unlawful devices and nets, to use as bait for eels and cod and also to feed their hogs, to the complete destruction of the said fry and spawn, unless a remedy is provided.[40]

The overwhelming concern for the Londoners thus seems to have been, not the loss of agricultural land around the Thames, but the perceived damage which flooding was having upon the river's fish stocks, through the placing of 'unlawful devices' – weirs or kiddles – in the flooded marshes to trap immature fish. The remedy sought was to grant the Mayor of London:

the conservation and rule, and the same authority in each of the said breaches, overflows and creeks and the drowned and flooded ground as far as the water is tidal, concerning the punishment for using unlawful nets and other unlawful devices in fishing, as he and his predecessors have had or have in the same water and river Thames...[41]

This strongly echoes concerns expressed a century earlier regarding the flooding of the marshlands at Barking, when a jury convened before the Mayor had found that the placing of weirs in the creeks of the flooded marsh was causing great damage to stocks, as fish entering through the great river-wall breach at high tide were trapped at the ebb.[42] Both are incidents in a long history of London concern with the regulation of the use of kiddles, weirs and other kinds of fixed devices in the Thames, both because of their potential harm to navigation and their potential to damage fish stocks.[43] What seems new in the later middle ages was the concern with flooded grounds beside the river, as well as with the main channel of the Thames itself.

A further piece of legislation, dating from 1535–6, shows that human actions were then suspected to have been as important as natural forces in causing flooding, and a more general deterioration of the condition of the Thames channel. The 'Acte for the Preservacion of the River of Thamyse' narrates how 'evil-disposed persons' had harmed the river through throwing dung and other rubbish into the channel, and through undermining the banks and walls of the river and carrying away 'piles, boards, timber work' and other parts of the actual river frontage.[44] The result of these actions, whether thoughtless or mischievous, had been that 'great shelpes [shelves] and risinges [floods] have of late been made and growen

[40] From: 'Henry VII: January 1489', *Parliament Rolls of Medieval England*. URL: <http://www.british-history.ac.uk/report.aspx?compid=116566&strquery=thames> accessed 29 May 2010.

[41] Ibid. The King granted the request, but excepted flooded lands owned by the Crown or forming part of franchises from the Mayor's jurisdiction, which may have rendered the expansion of the Londoners' powers largely useless.

[42] Galloway and Potts, 'Marine flooding', 374–5.

[43] D. Keene, 'Issues of water in medieval London', *Urban History* 21 (2008), 167–8.

[44] *Statutes of the Realm*, vol. 3, 550.

in the fareway of the said Ryver' and low-lying grounds had been 'surrounded and overflowen', and many great breaches had resulted. The river was likely to be 'utterly destroyed forever' if speedy action was not taken. This emphasis on the role of human agency in flooding is interesting, coming as it does at the time of the dissolution of the monasteries, and may be another reflection of the tendency for traditional practices and mechanisms for maintaining riverside defences to break down at a period of institutional upheaval and wholesale changes in land ownership.

London's interests in the riverside lands, and in the threat posed to them by marine flooding, thus seem by the close of the middle ages to have become largely confined to the issues of navigation and fisheries, whereas at an earlier period the marshlands had been important to the city as sources of agrarian produce – grain, meat, wool and dairy produce. This change reflects wider changes in economy and society after the Black Death, and in particular from the 1370s, when collapsing demand for bulk agricultural produce was translated into long-term price falls. At the same time, wages were inexorably rising, with dire consequences for the profitability of the Thames-side marshes.[45] These lands were highly productive, but were expensive to defend against the tides, and above all were prohibitively expensive to recover once storm flooding had breached riverside and coastal defences. At Barksore, a manor of Christ Church Canterbury near the mouth of the river Medway, expenditure on maintenance of marsh walls and ditches normally amounted to £2 or £3 per year, but in years when storm surges occurred – such as 1334 and the 1370s – could reach or exceed £30.[46] Such expenses were increasingly difficult to sustain. Consequently, it is in the post-Black Death period, and particularly from the 1370s onwards, that we begin to see significant examples of the *long-term loss or abandonment* of previously embanked land following storm-flooding. The change seems reflected in the pattern of issuing of commissions *de walliis et fossatis*, the mechanism by which the Crown empowered local landholders to compel the cooperation of neighbours in tackling flood threats and issues of drainage, which peak in the 1370s and decline thereafter, as attempts to defend all the reclaimed marshlands were gradually abandoned.[47]

Examples of adaptation to flooding by lords and tenants – developing fisheries, and harvesting other wild resources – have been cited above. Such activities, together with the grazing of sheep on salt-marsh, had characterised marshland exploitation before twelfth and thirteenth century embankment and drainage, and had continued on the minority of marshes which were never embanked, and on the foreland of saltmarsh and mudflats beyond river- and sea-walls. Now, from the later fourteenth century through to the early sixteenth century, they had once

---

[45] D.L. Farmer, 'Prices and wages', in E. Miller (ed.), *The Agrarian History of England and Wales* vol. 3, *1348–1500* (Cambridge 1991), 431–525.
[46] Galloway, 'Storm flooding', 14–17.
[47] Galloway, 'Storm flooding', 10–11.

again become the principal economic use of many marshlands. The later middle ages were a period when it simply did not make economic sense to maintain all the river- and sea-defences that had been built in an era of population growth and buoyant trade. Instead, retreat from 'hard' defence was a sensible response in many locations, allowing salt-marsh to regenerate and harvesting the resources it offered.

The situation of the Thames marshes at the close of the middle ages was thus highly complex. Where two centuries years earlier the picture had been one of general reclamation of the marshes, now they presented a patch-work; many reclaimed marshes continued to be used as agricultural land, defended against the tides, while others had reverted to inter-tidal conditions and their fisheries and other natural resources came to assume greater importance. Changes in the structure of demand from the London market – including a decline in the bulk grain trade and rising demand for fresh fish as living standards rose – had impacted upon the productive but vulnerable Thames marshes more intensely than elsewhere. The 1370s appear to represent a turning point in the history of the Thames marshes, after which the rapid repair of storm damaged sea- and river-defences was less likely to be the automatic response of marshland lords and communities. These conditions substantially persisted through the fifteenth century. In the sixteenth century, the dissolution of the monastic orders and the sometimes repeated changes of ownership that ensued added institutional disruption to the mix, and acted to prolong instances of flooding at some Thames-side locations. It was probably not until the second half of the sixteenth century, as London's population regained and then rapidly exceeded its peak medieval level, that the momentum for recovery of 'drowned marshes' became irresistible. Even then, as the example of Erith and Lesnes shows, technical difficulties, recurrent storms and the competing interests of Thames fishermen could still delay the renewed transformation of the marshland environment.

3. Floods and flood response in eighteenth-century London*

CARRY VAN LIESHOUT

Recent years have seen renewed attention to the flood risks that London faces as a result of its position on the Thames floodplain.[1] However, there is relatively little historical work on the occurrence of floods and the way that flooding was dealt with.[2] In this respect the eighteenth century is an especially under-researched period. Later developments in the nineteenth century, notably the construction of the docks, the new London Bridge and the embankments, profoundly changed London's waterscape and its flood prevention. However, flooding in the period prior to these alterations has received relatively little attention, despite the fact that during the eighteenth century London's built up area expanded significantly. There were issues relating to drainage and flooding that arose from the expansion of the built environment on the floodplain. This paper examines the relationships between the city and the environment by investigating flooding in eighteenth-century London, how floods affected people's lives and livelihoods and how they were dealt with. It attempts to quantify the scale of floods that took place and it explores the impact on the city and on people's lives.[3]

London's floods: causes, magnitude and frequency

Flooding in eighteenth-century London was a relatively common event, although the floods varied in both magnitude and frequency. The causes of large and small floods differed but they were always the result of a combination of natural and human factors. The city's location on the floodplain meant that flooding occurred naturally. However, human intervention altered the pattern of run-off and transformed the drainage. These changes, in conjunction with the physical processes associated with flooding, exacerbated the problem.

* This research is part of a PhD CASE award between King's College London and the Museum of London/Docklands. I am grateful to the Arts and Humanities Research Council for funding this research, and to David R. Green for his advice on this paper.

[1] For example: S. Lavery and B. Donovan, 'Flood risk management in the Thames Estuary looking ahead 100 years', *Philosophical Transactions of the Royal Society*, Series A, vol. 363, no. 1831 (2005), 1455–74.

[2] The most complete overview is A. Milne, *London's Drowning* (London, 1982), although it is mostly focused on the nineteenth and twentieth centuries.

[3] In this paper, when using 'London' or 'city', the old cities of London and Westminster, the borough of Southwark and the parishes that were built during the eighteenth century are included. When only the City of London is indicated, it will be fully spelled out and 'City' capitalised.

For the entire reach through London, the Thames is tidal and, until the main embankments were built in the mid nineteenth century, the river was much wider than today.[4] This tidal nature of the Thames was the most important cause of large scale flooding, often in combination with excessive rainfall and/or storms. Another main cause was a phenomenon called the 'surge', created when, through the funnelling effect of the North Sea, a large volume of water is forced into the mouth of the Thames and moves up the river like a tidal wave.[5] When the human systems designed to cope with these physical phenomena failed, flooding occurred. Excessive rainfall could lead to floods when water did not drain sufficiently quickly because of lower infiltration due to the expansion of the built up area; similarly, a spring tide or a surge would only become a flood if it was high enough to extend over the river's banks, or if it caused a breach in the river wall.[6] In addition, the old London Bridge, demolished in the early nineteenth century, was so solid it obstructed the tide and added to the flood risk both up and downstream.[7] In other words, floods are as much an indication of the failure of human systems as they are of extreme natural events.

The impact of floods depended primarily on their magnitude and frequency. Tidal flooding and storm surges were potentially the most destructive and far reaching but were relatively rare. Lower magnitude but higher frequency events in the form of localised small-scale floods, which affected only a street or a few houses, were less spectacular but not necessarily less important in relation to the day-to-day functions of a city. This type of flood was often due to structural defects in the sewer network, institutional delays in maintaining the sewers, 'freak' events such as burst water pipes or they were due to conflicting uses of water. There were innumerable instances of cellars and kitchens being flooded, either on individual occasions or as repeated events. These events were a relatively common experience for eighteenth-century Londoners, and, though rarely leading to loss of life, they were nevertheless important. Both types of flooding need to be considered in the context of urban growth during the eighteenth century.

London's eighteenth-century 'waterscape'

Any city on a floodplain is always prone to having an excess of standing water. Mapping the extent of this surface water, however, is by no means easy. Figure

[4] For an account of the construction of the Embankments, see: D.H. Porter, *The Thames Embankment, Environment, Technology, and Society in Victorian London* (Akron, Ohio, 1998).

[5] Milne, *London's Drowning*, 8–13, 32. See also the papers by Carlsson-Hyslop and Galloway in this volume.

[6] Not all river wall breaches were catastrophic: it was often done on purpose for industrial purposes, or for water supply. Chelsea Water Works made a thorough risk assessment before breaching the Millbank to let the water in: London Metropolitan Archives (LMA)/CH/1/1 minutes July/August 1725.

[7] J.H. Brazell, *London Weather* (Meteorological Office publication 783, London, 1968), 4. London suffered flooding two days after the 1703 storm, which had caused London Bridge to be blocked by loose ships and wreckage: H. Humpherus, *History of the Origin and Progress of the Company of Watermen and Lightermen of the river Thames with Numerous Historical Notes,* vol. 2 (Wakefield, 1981), 32.

FIG. 3.1. Surface water as evident on Rocque's 1746 London map.

3.1 outlines the extent of surface water shown on the 1746 Rocque map of London.[8]

Using GIS, all visible water features have been traced and are depicted here. These features include the Thames and tributaries, open sewers, docks, canals and ponds. It does not show, however, the network of water pipes that existed in certain parts of the city nor the covered sewers. Figure 3.1 shows that standing water was commonplace in eighteenth-century London primarily in southern districts that were lower-lying and marshier than those to the north. Other poorly drained areas included the land south of Westminster, which is now Pimlico and Victoria station. These areas were more prone to flooding and there were more issues relating to land drainage.

In eighteenth-century London, surface water was channelled via a gutter and kennel system into ditches and streams and eventually flowed into the Thames. In theory at least, this system could deal with the normal amount of surface water. In bad weather and rain, however, the excess water posed a challenge to the system and the water would overflow into cellars and lower levels.[9]

Evidence of large scale floods

There were no consistent instrumental weather observations before 1841 and therefore the record of flooding has to be pieced together from a variety of sources.[10]

---

[8] J. Rocque, *A Plan of the Cities of London and Westminster, and Borough of Southwark; with the Contiguous Buildings* (1746).

[9] E. Cockayne, *Hubbub: Filth, Noise and Stench in England 1600–1770* (London, 2007), 191–2.

[10] Brazell, *London Weather*, 1.

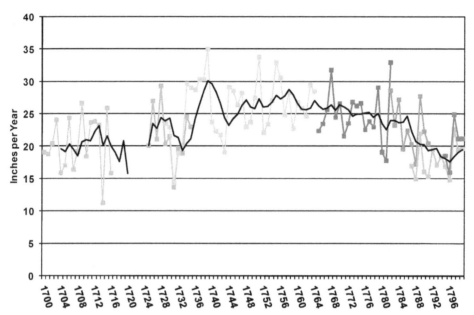

Fig. 3.2. Rainfall in inches per year in and around London in the
eighteenth century, with moving average.
(Source: based on data in Brazell, *London Weather*, appendix II)

The number and detail of records available improved for the second half of the
eighteenth century, as interest in the measurement of natural events was fostered
by the Enlightenment.[11] There were no official meteorological records, although a
few series from various places in (and around) London have survived and suggest,
on average, wetter circumstances between approximately 1740–1780 (Fig. 3.2).[12]

Large scale floods were relatively rare but in general were better documented
than the low magnitude but high frequency small scale flooding. There is no
definitive record of all London floods, and the evidence presented here has been
compiled from different sources. Most evidence of large scale floods was found in
J.H. Brazell's *London Weather*, which includes a compilation of floods derived from
various historical sources.[13] The second main source is H. Humpherus's history of
the Watermen's Company, in which he tracked important events on and off the river
Thames, as well as general facts related to weather, water, the Thames and its banks.[14]

---

[11] J. Golinski, *British Weather and the Climate of Enlightenment* (Chicago, 2007), xiii.

[12] See also: Brazell, *London Weather*, 4; H.H. Lamb, *Climate, History and the Modern World*
(London, 1982), 231–6.

[13] Brazell's main sources for the eighteenth century were: E.J. Lowe, *Natural Phenomena and
Chronology of the Seasons* (London, 1870), and a manuscript by G. Manley, 'Daily meteorological
observations for the London area 1723–1805'.

[14] This is mostly based on the Watermen's Company's own records, although Humpherus has
used a variety of other historical sources as well. Most floods have been found in both Brazell and
Humpherus, and some may have been derived from the same sources.

The main cause, or causes, of a flood were often recorded as well, although here again there was more and better data for the latter part of the century. While it should be realised that not all large floods might be in these records, they have been the most extensive compilations of floods and weather found so far, although research is still ongoing.

Using these sources, 40 floods were identified, with varying amounts of detail.

TABLE 3.1. Large scale floods in London 1700–1799

Year	Date (if known)	Specific location	Characteristics
1703	28 November		Tidal flood after destructive storm on 26 Nov 1703
1726	8 March		Thames 4 inches higher than normal
1728	February		Very high tide caused floording
1731	31 December	Wapping, Tooley	Cellars and warehouses flooded
1735	8 January		Flooding due to snow, waterside premises suffer
1736	16 February	Westminster/Southwark	Severe flooding after strong spring tide
1736	24 December	Westminster/Tothill Fields	Severe flooding after breach in Millbank
1740	1 November		Violent hurricane caused great inundation of the Thames
1747	24 October	Tooley, Barnaby	Extraordinary spring tide
1749	31 January		High winds and floods, many lives lost
1750	11 July		Thunderstorms with hail caused flooding
1750	24 July		Thunderstorms with hail caused flooding
1751	21 November		Thunderstorms with hail and snow caused flooding
1753	22 March	Whitehall	Floods
1754	13 December		High tide. Cellars adjoining river flooded
1762	12 January		Water higher than known in many years, flooding
1762	9 February	Rotherhithe, Dockhead	High tide, cellars and warehouses flooded
1762	22 March	Westminster Hall	High tide
1762	27 October		High tide and incessant rain, water high in houses
1763	29 January	All along the Thames	Floods on melting ice, severe inundations
1763	13–15 February	Westminster/Southwark	High tides, severe damage due to flood
1763	2 December		Storm and high tide over the banks
1764	28 September		High tide inundated houses on both banks
1767	2 January		Hurricane caused floods
1767	4 June		Heavy rain for 3 days with high tides
1768	10 September	Thames, Serpentine, Fleet	Land floods due to heaviest rain
1768	1 December	Thames, Lea	Very heavy rains make a high tide overflow banks
1772	22 March		Storm and rain cause flood
1773	19 August		Storm with rainwater, many streets impassable
1774	12 March	Chelsea and Battersea	Excessive rains made the tide overflow
1775	1 February	Below (London) Bridge	Violent storms and rains
1775	6 February	Westminster Hall	More than a foot of water
1783	31 August	Fleet, Buckingham House	Floods in storm
1785	13 March		Remarkable high tide damages cellars
1791	2 February	Westminster/Blackwall	Highest floods in years, heavy rains and springtide
1794	7 August		Rain and hail sotrms, banks overflow
1795	mid Feburary		Floods following the breaking ice
1796	12 February		Strong tide overflowed banks, cellars flooded
1796	3 December	Tooley	Tide overflowed banks, warehouses flooded
1798	7 November	South London	All levels inundated

Sources: Brazell, *London Weather*, appendix I and Humpherus, *Watermen and Lightermen.*

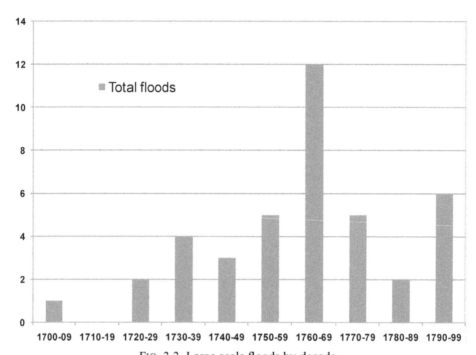

FIG. 3.3. Large scale floods by decade.
(Sources: Brazell, *London Weather*, appendix I and Humpherus, *Watermen and Lightermen)*

TABLE 3.2. Large scale floods by decade and (partial) cause: rain and tidal
For some floods no causes were recorded and other floods
were caused by a combination of both rain and tide.

Decade	Total floods	Cause/partial cause	
		Rain	Tidal
1700–9	1		1
1710–19	0		
1720–9	2		2
1730–9	4	1	2
1740–9	3	2	1
1750–9	5	3	1
1760–9	12	6	9
1770–9	5	4	
1780–9	2	1	1
1790–9	6	2	3

Sources: Brazell, *London Weather,* appendix I and Humpherus, *Watermen and Lightermen.*

These were unevenly distributed throughout the century. When broken down by decade, it becomes evident that there was more flooding in the second half of the century, and especially in the 1760s, which saw four floods in 1762 alone. This difference between the first half of the century and second half can be explained in a number of ways: change in recording, change in climate and change in topography. Firstly, the before-mentioned rise in interest in the recording of natural events during the second half of the century implies that the failure to note earlier floods, may, in part, be a result of the lack of recording.

Secondly, the British climate is thought to have become wetter during the second half of the eighteenth century (Fig. 3.2), thus causing flooding as a result of run-off. Indeed, Table 3.2 shows that more floods in the second half of the century were due to rain (including snow and hailstorms), or partly due to rain, whereas the number of tide-based floods stayed relatively stable, with the 1760s a notable exception. Weather and rainfall records for the London area at this time are unfortunately very sketchy and it should be remembered that the data used to compute Figure 3.2 are far from rigorous.

A third explanation for the increase in floods in the second half of the eighteenth century is an expansion of the built up area. London expanded from approximately 675,000 people in 1750 to 900,000 in the 1801 census, and most of the West End was built during this time. In addition, south London started to be developed following the construction of Westminster and Blackfriars bridges in 1750 and 1769.[15] To sum up, the rise in floods evident in the second half of the eighteenth century could have been caused by changes in recording, climate change or changes in the built-up areas. It is likely to have been a combination of all three causes.

Evidence of smaller scale floods

Evidence of the low magnitude, high frequency floods has been taken from the available records of the several commissions of sewers in the London area.[16] The commissions of sewers, discussed more fully below, were in charge of flood defence and drainage. Throughout the eighteenth century there was no single regulatory body for greater London responsible for the sewers. Instead there were seven separate commissions for the following districts: City of London, Westminster, Holborn and Finsbury, Tower Hamlets, Poplar, Surrey and Kent and St Katherine.[17] The minutes of their meetings have been preserved and are available at the London Metropolitan Archives (LMA). Due to the huge quantity of these records, only the years ending in –2 have been sampled, showing one year each decade per commission.[18] However, only the Surrey and Kent and City of London commissions provided a continuous record for all decades. Holborn and

---

[15] S. Inwood, *A History of London* (London, 2000), 258.

[16] These are: City of London, Westminster, Surrey and Kent, Holborn and Finsbury, and Tower Hamlets. The Poplar commission's records are in such a poor condition they could not be consulted, and St. Katherine did not have records available for these years.

[17] I. Darlington, 'The London Commissioners of Sewers and their Records', in F. Ranger (ed.), *Prisca Munimenta* (London, 1973), 283; F. Hargrave, *The Law of Sewers* (London, 1732), 25–6.

[18] Sampling ensured that it was feasible to look at a broad coverage of all commissions over a long time period.

Finsbury, Tower Hamlets and Westminster have gaps in the records arising from the failure of a commission to function or meet or because of the poor state or absence of records.[19] In the minute books of the sampled years, only specific mentions of cellars, houses, kitchens, grounds or roads being flooding, water returning into houses or foundations damaged by water have been counted. Not included are mentions of the sewer being stopped up with mud and the need for cleansing (although this would often have caused floods), or residents being 'annoyed' due to stopped up sewers. Also excluded are the many applications for private drains to be connected to the sewers, unless it was specifically mentioned that it was to aid the drainage of water from springs.[20] This means that it is highly probable that there were more floods recorded in these minutes, and the actual number of floods that occurred in London is therefore likely to have been higher.

TABLE 3.3 Small scale floods in London 1702–1792, every 10 years

Year	City of London	Westminster	Holborn & Finsbury	Tower Hamlets	Surrey & Kent	Total London
1702	2	8	n/a	n/a	1	11
1712	n/a	11	n/a	0	1	12
1722	4	23	10	n/a	2	39
1732	8	8	10	2	0	28
1742	9	14	15	1	1	40
1752	10	9	8	2	0	29
1762	6	9	n/a	6	0	21
1772	7	24	3	n/a	0	34
1782	8	n/a	0	n/a	0	8
1792	4	n/a	0	0	0	4
Total	**58**	**106**	**46**	**11**	**5**	**226**

Sources: LMA/WCS/45–60, LMA/SKCS/42–56, LMA/HFCS/13–18, LMA/THCS/10–18, LMA/CLA/006/AD/003–019 and LMA/CLA/006/AD/04/09–29.

Table 3.3 shows the number of small scale flooding incidents for all commissions throughout the eighteenth century. Most mentions of flood were in Westminster and the City of London, which were the most built-up areas.[21] Some of the commissions which operated in areas prone to flooding, such as the Surrey and Kent Commission, did not really record many instances of this type of flood. The lack of reporting in these areas may have resulted from greater acceptance that flooding was a normal part of life, or it could reflect the inefficiency of the commission. It could also reflect the fact that with more open ground, water could drain away better and therefore was less of a nuisance. That flooding did occur

[19] Westminster has been excluded from the last two decades as their organizational structure changed, and the subcommittee dealing with the practical issues was not included in the main records included in this sample.

[20] See, for example, Little Britain, City of London, cellars flooded in 1742: LMA, CLA/006/AD/03/12 on 09/04/1742.

[21] Work on more specific geography is in progress.

is evident in years outside those sampled in this research. In 1735, for example, it was mentioned that several sluices were defective and many of the properties protected by those sluices were frequently overflowed.[22] Some evidence for greater acceptance of flooding can be found in a case of 1707, when Earl Sluice level inhabitants complained that with the winter approaching the level was in danger of land floods coming from the hills, which had frequently happened. When the Surrey and Kent Commission asked why they had never complained about this before, they answered that they never had received so much damage before. This indicates that they were used to flooding up to a certain degree, but appealed to the commission when floods caused too much damage.[23]

Despite the fact that the number of flood incidents has been conservatively estimated, and that each 'count' may indicate an ongoing flooding problem at a certain location, rather than a single flood incident, it appears that flooding was a common nuisance during the eighteenth century throughout London. It seems that residents would apply to the commission when their area had been flooded more than once or even on a regular basis: the phrase 'in sudden rains' or 'in heavy rains' or 'in the wet season' is often used to indicate when the flooding occurs. There was, of course, considerable variation in the length of time between the problem first showing up and it being brought to court: there were instances of people complaining to court the next day, or after a month or two months of experiencing a flooding nuisance.[24] In addition, while some courts met every one or two weeks, some only met four times a year, which would delay any actions taken to alleviate the problem.[25]

The main cause of the smaller floods was sewers being stopped up with mud, dirt and filth. The next most common cause was structural problems in the sewer system, such as a sewer lying higher than the cellars of nearby residents, the gullyhole in the street being too narrow to convey all the water, or a street having been repaved and raised which altered the flow of water.[26] Occasionally, the issue was the result of conflicting usages of waterways and so the flooding was ultimately due to the actions of other inhabitants. In several cases, these conflicting usages referred to rivers which in turn impacted on residents and businesses along their watercourses. The river Wandle, for

---

[22] LMA, SKCS/44 on 22/01/1735.

[23] LMA, SKCS/42 on 25/09/1707.

[24] Long Alley residents went the day after they had been surprised in the night by floods, LMA/HFCS/17 on 21/05/1742; and Duke Street inhabitants had had their cellar two feet under water for two months, when they petitioned on 12/11/1742, LMA, WCS/53.

[25] There is no solid data in the minutes on the time passing between applying to court and the issue being solved as the commissions did not keep track of this in their records.

[26] A high sewer was the cause of cellars in Lombard Street flooding in 1742: LMA, CLA/006/AD/03/12 on 22/10/1742. An example of a narrow gullyhole can be found in LMA, CLA/006/AD/03/16 on 01/05/1752. Yards were overflowing in Fetter Lane because it had been repaved: LMA, CLA/006/AD/04/19 on 30/07/1782.

example, was reported to have been obstructed by dams for industrial use on several occasions, which caused floods upstream, and this sort of obstruction occurred in a sewer in the Westminster commission as well.[27] John Owen constructed a road over a sewer in Bethnal Green, thereby blocking it up, which flooded the houses north of this road, and in Poplar somebody cut a hole in the sewer wall letting the foul water flow over Jeremiah Wade's land.[28] Sometimes the cause of a flood was something as simple as directing a spout onto a neighbour's pavement and flooding it, as Sarah Fortescue of Fleet Street complained in 1762.[29] The commissioners of sewers usually dealt with this by ordering the obstruction to be removed.

Consequences and experiences of being flooded

The effects, and people's experiences of floods in eighteenth-century London largely depended on the scale and type of flood as well as the area affected. None of the sample of smaller scale floods mentioned any loss of human life, whereas some of the larger floods resulted in the deaths of both people and animals. Mentions of loss of life through flooding were not uncommon; for example, 22 people drowned in London in the 1703 storm and flood.[30] Many lives were lost in the storms of 1749 and in an 'extraordinary tide' exacerbated by rain in October 1762 all waterside property was damaged and people were drowned.[31] Similarly, the loss of animals was a repeated consequence of large scale flooding. Cattle drowned in a January 1735 flood in which riverside premises were damaged after the melting of snow.[32] In the October 1762 rains, cattle were washed away and, according to Humpherus, an estimated 50,000 pigs were lost.[33] When the Fleet river overtopped its banks in a storm in 1783 more than 1,000 sheep and pigs were said to be 'floating around'.[34]

The smaller scale floods generally affected people only in 'hasty rains' in their 'cellars and kitchens'.[35] The water could rise fast: people affected by the Long Alley sewer in Holborn in 1742 were frightened out of their beds by the incoming

---

[27] For an example of Wandle obstruction and the way the Surrey and Kent commission dealt with it, see LMA, SKCS/43, on 13/09/1722 and 16/10/1722. For the Westminster sewer, see LMA, WCS/45 of 19/02/1701/2.

[28] LMA, THCS/15 meeting on 18/02/1762 and LMA, THCS/14 on 05/03/1752.

[29] LMA, CLA/006/AD/03/19 on 08/10/1762.

[30] Milne, London's Drowning, 20.

[31] Humpherus, Watermen and Lightermen, 253.

[32] Humpherus, Watermen and Lightermen, 152.

[33] Humpherus, Watermen and Lightermen, 253. This number possibly included the whole Thames estuary, and might have been exaggerated.

[34] Humpherus, Watermen and Lightermen, 359.

[35] This is the general formula used by the Westminster commission when recording petitions for floods, with variations on e.g. roads, grounds or only cellars flooded. All other commissions had similar formulas.

water, and found their belongings afloat.[36] Occasionally there is mention of roads made impassable by the water, causing a nuisance for the inhabitants as well as passers-by.[37] Material damage arising from these small scale floods usually consisted of the goods stored in vaults and cellars, though details were rarely recorded except when the owner was a landlord of a public house and kept valuable stock there. Other material damage consisted of water damage to the foundations of the house, or houses being left 'useless' or 'not fit for habitation' after prolonged exposure to water, which mainly occurred where sewers were absent.[38]

Large scale floods brought material damage on a greater scale, particularly in areas where wharfs and warehouses were close to the river. For example on 31 December 1731, a flood in Wapping and Tooley Street overflowed cellars and warehouses on both sides of the river, 'spoiling merchandize' there.[39] With a high tide in February 1762, warehouses flooded in Rotherhithe and Dockhead. One year later high tides caused an estimated £20,000 damage to goods in warehouses in these riverside areas.[40] Residents had to remain on the upper floors as many houses were five feet under water.[41] A particularly high tide in December 1796 destroyed foreign wheat supplies in the Tooley Street warehouses.[42]

Individual localities were sometimes prone to repeated flooding. Westminster Hall, for example, was flooded on several occasions during the century. It was flooded twice during spring tides in 1736. In February of that year a committee had been discussing the possible construction of what would become Westminster Bridge, and the flood was perceived by some as a reminder of the changes in the river that a bridge could bring about.[43] In 1762 the water came all the way to the stairs leading to the House of Commons, and a year later there was four feet of water inside the Hall.[44] More than a foot of water stood in the Hall in 1775.[45] People had to be transported by boats on several occasions as the streets were impassable.[46] After the 1791 spring tide, Westminster Hall and Palace Yard were inaccessible for two hours until the water abated again, and there was a scuffle for boats with people being thrown into the water.[47]

[36] LMA, HFCS/17 on 21/05/1742.
[37] Especially the Holborn and Finsbury commission records this, see for an example LMA, HFCS/14 on 11/07/1722.
[38] For an example, see the petition of residents of Aldersgate in LMA, CLA/006/AD/04/19 on 17/12/1782.
[39] Humpherus, *Watermen and Lightermen,* 145.
[40] Humpherus, *Watermen and Lightermen,* 249, 255.
[41] Humpherus, *Watermen and Lightermen,* 255.
[42] Humpherus, *Watermen and Lightermen,* 420.
[43] Humpherus, *Watermen and Lightermen,* 153–4.
[44] Humpherus, *Watermen and Lightermen,* 249, 255.
[45] Humpherus, *Watermen and Lightermen,* 311.
[46] E.g. Humpherus, *Watermen and Lightermen,* 200.
[47] Humpherus, *Watermen and Lightermen,* 380–1.

The institutional response

London's flood defence was officially entrusted to the commissioners of sewers, first introduced as *ad hoc* bodies in the thirteenth century, but given more permanent power during the Tudor period to protect the country from encroachment by the sea, river or streams. Over the years they had acquired another official function, namely, to drain water from the land. Regardless of the modern meaning of their name, they were not supposed to concern themselves with wastewater, although they did drain kitchen and household water. In fact, connecting toilets to the sewers was illegal, and the word 'sewer' in this case referred to a man-made drainage channel, and included gutters and kennels.[48] The river Thames had its own commission from the late 1770s, the Thames Navigation Committee, as well as the Thames Conservancy Courts throughout the century which took care of the river and encroachments on its banks.

The several commissions of sewers in the London area had jurisdiction over all river walls and banks, as well as ditches, sewers, streams and watercourses. They were established and operated as separate entities, each under their own statute and with slightly different powers and ways of governing their district. They were initially established for a fixed number of years, after which their mandate ran out and was either immediately renewed or a new mandate was sought after a certain time.[49] In the eighteenth century, only the City of London and Westminster had a permanent commission; all other areas had gaps in between the separate commissions (although a new commission would take over the accounts and minutes of the old one, and often consisted of the same people as well). Their areas varied greatly in character, which influenced the kind of issues they faced. The City of London was a completely built up area, Tower Hamlets was still largely rural and Surrey and Kent and Westminster had a mix of densely built as well as more rural areas.[50]

In practice, the main part of their business consisted of maintaining, cleaning and deepening sewers, and maintaining sluices for the lower lying areas, as well as negotiating with landlords and developers who wanted to connect new drains. They met on a regular basis in a 'court' setting in which people brought petitions. As they were responsible for preventing flooding they had the power to fine or amerce people who did not comply with their orders. They were entitled to tax everyone who either benefited from, or avoided damage due to their work. These taxes were their main source of income.[51]

---

[48] Darlington, 'London Commissioners of Sewers', 283; Hargrave, *The Law of Sewers*, 25–26.

[49] Darlington, 'London Commissioners of Sewers', 283.

[50] S. and B. Webb, *English Local Government from the Revolution to the Municipal Corporations Act, Volume IV: Statutory Authorities for Special Purposes* (London, 1922), 58.

[51] C.M., *The Laws of Sewers* (London 1762), 13, 15–16.

How did the commissioners of sewers react to these floods?[52] In the case of small scale floods, the commissioners' attention was drawn to the problem by residents petitioning them to do something about the nuisance, after which the commissioners viewed the matter and determined the response. At their next meeting, the course of action (usually cleaning and/or repairing the sewer) was decided on and depending whether it was a public or a private sewer the commission would fix it themselves and retrieve the money via a tax, or would order the sewer to be fixed at the residents' costs under their supervision.[53] Residents without any sewer generally applied to the court as well, and if there were enough new houses to make it worthwhile to build a new sewer the commission would usually comply. In general, however, the commissions were reactive rather than proactive in taking initiatives themselves.

Their primary function, however, was to protect London from inundation by sea or river, and thus we should look at their reaction to the large scale floods.[54] Most of the large floods featured in Table 3.1 that were due to high tides are not mentioned in the minutes, or only touched on briefly if the commissioners went to take a view of the river walls.[55] This suggests that they only sprang into action if there was a breach in the flood defences. One such breach occurred on 24 December 1736 in the Millbank. Behind this river wall is the low lying marshy area of Tothill fields, which flooded on this occasion, north of which is the City of Westminster. The Westminster Commission of Sewers was warned and called an emergency meeting in which they noted that it was a serious breach which, unless it was stopped, could cause a general flooding of Westminster within one or two high tides – which basically meant 12 to 24 hours.[56]

What followed in the records seems to represent some kind of improvised disaster management: the six commissioners who came to view the breach appointed someone on the spot as surveyor, and hired as many workers as possible at short notice. They ordered a Mr Price to get as many barges loaded with dung as he could to stop the breach. They generally used other material such as clay and it is possible that this time they used dung as it was close to hand at a nearby

---

[52] The efficiency of the Commissioners of Sewers in the early nineteenth century has recently been the subject of attention, although the main focus was on their financial and legal competence rather than their ways of dealing with floods. See D. Sunderland, '"A monument to defective administration"? The London Commissioners of Sewers in the early nineteenth century', *Urban History* 26, (1999); P. Jefferson-Smith, 'Before Bazalgette: the Surrey and Kent Commission of Sewers, 1800–1847', *Transactions of the Newcomen Society*, 74 (2004) and J.G. Hanley, 'The Metropolitan Commissioners of Sewers and the law, 1812–1847', *Urban History* 33 (2006).

[53] The distinction between private and public sewers was not always clear cut, and depended mostly on precedent.

[54] All of the large scale floods in table 1 have been searched for in the minutes of the commissioners, not only those in the years ending in –2.

[55] As the Surrey and Kent commission did as recorded in their 30/10/1722 meeting: LMA/SKCS/43.

[56] LMA, WCS/53 reported in meeting on 21/01/1736/7.

wharf, and they needed anything they could find to stop this breach quickly. A full meeting of all commissioners was called on 28 December, four days after the initial breach, and they heard that the river wall was expected to be up to its former height by the New Year.

The commission tried to examine whose fault the breach was and heard evidence from a neighbour who had known the river wall for twenty-two years. He claimed that another breach had occurred earlier that year (probably during the June 1736 flood of Westminster Hall, included in Table 3.1) in the same spot and that it had not been effectually repaired by Mr Harvey, who occupied the land; and that the water had at times oozed through the bank, which had also been overtopped by spring tides. This Mr Harvey seemed to have been blamed for the breach, as he had not repaired the first break properly, although there is no record of him being ordered to repair it by the commission and neither is there mention of any punishment.[57] Eventually, the earl of Somerset reluctantly paid for the repairs; as the owner of the land he was the one who suffered most from the damage and benefited most from the commissioners' work.[58]

This case raises a few questions. Why did the commissioners not deal with this first breach themselves? Why, if neighbours knew that Mr Harvey's repairs were not well executed, and could witness that, did they not apply to the Commissioners of Sewers themselves? Once again, the commissioners seem more reactive than proactive.

Accountability

In both types of flooding the commissioners did not appear to have been effective at preventing floods, but merely dealt with damage control when something happened. As they were the ones responsible for preventing the land from flooding and for draining it, did they feel any responsibility when it went wrong, or did people hold them accountable for it?

On some occasions it seems that people felt the commissions were to blame if they were affected by a flood. In January 1707 a great breach occurred in the common sewer in Castle Street, St Martin in the Fields. One of the inhabitants there, a victualler called John Kendrick, asked for compensation for his spoiled stock – 4 butts of beer and a large box of tobacco – as the water from the breach had run into his vaults. While he estimated the whole damage to come to over £10, the commissioners gave him just £3 raised from the taxes.[59] In 1712 Nicholas Figg's vaults were flooded and the water spoiled his goods. He incurred large expense emptying it, which he tried to reclaim from the Westminster Commission. After an investigation they found that their workmen had cut through a pipe while

---

[57] LMA, WCS/53 reported in meeting on 21/01/1736/7.
[58] LMA, WCS/53 on 27/05/1737.
[59] LMA, WCS/47 on 02/09/1707.

repairing a sewer and a lot of water had escaped. They agreed that Mr Figg should be compensated £3 from the taxes raised to pay for those repairs.[60] This shows that the commissioners felt some degree of accountability for the failure of the sewer system.

However, when a commission decided that they had not neglected their duty they refused to pay any compensation. John Gibbs, a dealer in cider and Ramsbury beer, had £200 of his stock ruined in several vaults in Curzon Street, Mayfair. The sewer next to his vaults had been in a bad condition for a long time and when the commission's delegates came to inspect it, the sewer broke. While he held the commission responsible for this, the commissioners themselves ruled against him and he did not receive any compensation.[61]

Although the commissioners sometimes took responsibility for their actions, in general it was felt that they were not very effective. In 1778 a petition was sent to the House of Commons by owners and tenants of lands and meadows adjoining the Thames, stating that the laws in force for preventing floods were inadequate, and that great injury was done to their land. They asked for the laws to be amended to enable commissioners to more effectively prevent floods.[62] It is perhaps no coincidence that this petition came after some of the wettest years of the century. Nothing seems to have resulted from the petition and landowners and tenants would have to wait until the mid nineteenth century until measures to improve the flood defences were taken.

In conclusion, during the eighteenth century London experienced numerous instances of small scale as well as large scale flooding. The low magnitude, high frequency events were a nuisance but little more than that. The floods arising from storm surges or breaches in the river walls were altogether more serious. These kinds of events appeared to increase later in the century, possibly as a result of climate change as well as human interference in the natural hydrological regime. Responses to these different kinds of events differed, though the commissions tended to be more reactive than proactive in the way they anticipated problems. In the early nineteenth century, the position of the commissioners came under fire for their inefficiency and they were amalgamated as the Metropolitan Commission of Sewers in 1848. The Thames, meanwhile, continued to threaten London until the Thames Barrier put an end to this (for now) with its completion in 1982.

---

[60] LMA, WCS/48 on 26/08/1712.
[61] LMA, WCS/53 on 26/02/1741/2.
[62] Humpherus, *Watermen and Lightermen*, 332.

4.   Storm surge science: the London connection 1928–1953*

ANNA CARLSSON-HYSLOP

At 1 a.m. on Saturday 7 January 1928 a depression in the North Sea sent a storm surge through the heart of London. Or, in words used at the time, the storm winds produced an 'abnormal' and 'extraordinary' rise in sea level at about the same time as the high water of a springtide, which led to the highest river levels seen in the Thames for fifty years.[1] The flood defences along the Thames were designed to withstand a tide of 18 feet above Ordnance Datum, a height decided on after a previous record tide, reaching 17 feet 6 inches, had caused flooding in 1881. The height of the tide on 7 January 1928 exceeded this previous record by 11 inches. The flood defences were overtopped and broken through in several places with water flowing fast into basement rooms near the Thames. Many poor families slept in such basement rooms and 14 people drowned.[2] There was flooding in the City, Westminster, Southwark and less central areas, including Putney and Hammersmith.[3] Thousands of homes were damaged.[4] Most of the poor living in basement flats were uninsured and the insurance of many businesses did not cover floods.[5] There was no pre-existing warning system, and it seems warnings and the immediate rescue and relief operation were organised spontaneously. On Saturday morning after the flooding existing organisations ground into action, with large scale aid organised by many public and private agencies.[6]

---

* This paper is based on research I am doing for my PhD studies at the Centre for History of Science, Technology and Medicine at the University of Manchester, funded by the Economic and Social Research Council. I would like to thank the participants of the conference 'London, the Thames and Water' and the CHSTM lunch-time seminar and especially my supervisors Jeff Hughes and James Sumner for very helpful comments on various versions of this paper.

[1] S.T.A. Mirrlees, 'The Thames floods of January 7th', *The Meteorological Magazine* (1928).

[2] J.G. Gibbon, 'Report of a committee appointed at a conference of Public Authorities to consider the question of floods from the River Thames in the County of London', in *Command Papers; Reports of Commissioners* (1928), 8.

[3] Mirrlees, 'The Thames floods of January 7th', 17.

[4] 'London's Peril Not yet Over', *Guardian*, January 9 1928, 'Plight of Victims of the Flood,' *Daily Mirror*, January 9 1928.

[5] 'Our London Correspondence', *Guardian*, January 9 1928.

[6] 'Public Buildings Shelter Homeless', *Guardian*, January 9 1928, 'Pitiable Scenes at Westminster', *Observer*, January 8 1928, 'Relief Fund Opened', *Observer*, January 8 1928, 'The London Flood A', *Times*, January 9 1928.

This event prompted scientific research into storm surges, with a first round of research quickly given funding. However, a second investigation was delayed for almost a decade in wrangles over funding. Why? What was it about the funding for this particular small scientific inquiry that made it become such a contentious issue? It was linked to the question of who should pay for flood defence; a wider question which has had different answers at different times.

The event fed into pre-existing concerns regarding issues ranging from land drainage to the plight of the poor living in basement slum dwellings.[7] The event also became a focus for already on-going debates regarding how to govern London. For example, calls for an inquiry into the event by London-based Labour members were part of their demands for reforms: not just social reforms, such as banning basement dwellings, but also political reforms to London's local government with London Labour wanting a 'real Corporation of London' instead of the multitude of councils that existed.[8] In particular the event became a focus for debates regarding how to govern flood defence policy: who should organise and pay for flood defence in the capital? More generally, should flood defence be seen as a local responsibility or as a national issue? To what extent should national government be involved with flood defence? At this time flood defence was seen as a local issue. While the London County Council (LCC) had an overview role in London, the defences were paid for by the owners of the defended riverside land.

The key question for this paper is how the patronage of storm surge science in this period became entangled with London-based power struggles about who should be responsible for flood defence. A first round of research was quickly given funding by local/regional London government, but a second round of research did not begin until 1938, as the funding become entangled both in debates regarding how London should be governed and in debates between local government and central government. The paper will first look at the local debates and then at the debates with central government regarding funding for the research. Central government was repeatedly asked to fund surge science, but refused, claiming it was not of national interest but that flood defence should remain a local responsibility and cost. The Treasury's view of flood defence as a local responsibility was upheld and two regional authorities, the LCC and the Port of London Authority (PLA), were the key financial patrons of storm surge science in the UK at the time. However, the Second World War and another coastal flood in 1953, in which over 300 people drowned on the east coast, changed all this,

---

[7] For more on how the event was discussed, see A. Carlsson, 'What is a storm: severe weather and public life in Britain in January 1928', in V. Jankovic and C. Barboza (eds.), *Weather, Local Knowledge and Everyday Life: Issues in Integrated Climate Studies* (Rio de Janeiro, 2009).

[8] 'Labour Demand for Inquiry', *Times*, January 12 1928. See also 'Responsibility for Floods', *Guardian*, January 12 1928.

shifting patronage of storm surge science towards central government, which had earlier strongly contested such a shift.

The first round of storm surge research

The 1928 flooding event led to media attention on flood defence policy and to flood science. Ungar has argued that such media attention after an extreme event can be an important trigger for scientific research, and this happened after the 1928 event.[9] In response to demands in the newspapers and Parliament for an inquiry into the event, the Prime Minister, Stanley Baldwin, invited national, regional and local government actors within the LCC area to a conference 'to settle what action can, and should, be taken to obviate any recurrence of such […] disaster'. The Conservative Prime Minister side-stepped issues of blame and criticisms regarding the governance of London and the plight of the poor by emphasising future prevention: 'The object of the conference is not to discuss the responsibility for the incidents of last week-end, but to consider steps that should prevent a recurrence.'[10] Baldwin framed the event as 'just' about flooding, not about London governance or poverty-reduction. The conference was chaired by the Ministry of Health. At this time this Ministry was the government department that dealt with local government and supervised local authorities, so the choice of the Ministry of Health as the coordinating body for the conference mirrored and strengthened the existing allocation of responsibility for flood defence to local government.[11]

The media paid attention to a range of issues, especially the re-building and strengthening of physical flood defences and the lack of warnings. The Ministry of Health conference regarding the event was attended by local and regional authorities and a range of government departments and it quickly set up a Technical Sub-Committee to look further into such questions and also questions regarding the causes and frequency of surges. The Technical Sub-Committee consisted of representatives from the Admiralty's Hydrographic Department, the Meteorological Office, the PLA, the Thames Conservancy, the Ministry of Health and the Board of Trade. At this point the Thames Conservancy was the body responsible for the non-tidal Thames, but before 1909 it had also been responsible for the tidal river downstream of Teddington. This had been taken over by the PLA on its formation. Though this Sub-Committee agreed that the main cause of the flooding event was an unusually high tide due to meteorological effects, the details of the process leading to such 'abnormal' tides were not clear to them. Furthermore, it was thought that the frequency and height of future floods could

---

[9] S. Ungar, 'The rise and (relative) decline of global warming as a social problem', *The Sociological Quarterly* 33, no. 4 (1992).

[10] 'Prevention of Floods', *Times*, January 13 1928.

[11] *Whitaker's Almanack* (London, 1930), 516.

not be estimated until this process was better understood, which in turn meant that the benefits of increasing the flood defences could not be compared to the costs.[12] While a warning system was immediately set up for the Thames, the Technical Sub-Committee of the conference claimed that more research was needed to improve this system.[13] The desire to estimate the cost of flood defences and also to improve the warning system were key reasons behind the scientific work on storm surges that followed this flood.

These were new concerns for the organisation that was picked to do the research, which was the Liverpool Tidal Institute (LTI, now the National Oceanographic Centre, Liverpool). LTI had started in 1919 with funding primarily from Liverpool shipping men, though it had also been given grants by the British Association for the Advancement of Science and the Department for Scientific and Industrial Research. It had been established in a context where the increasing size of ships and the First World War had created an industrial and military demand for increasingly accurate tidal predictions, and its early work had concentrated on improving the accuracy of such astronomically-based predictions. LTI had also done work on 'meteorological effects' on sea level, focusing on providing formulae to 'correct' astronomically-based tidal predictions for the effect of wind and barometric pressure. Their work on storm surge science had thus been aimed at aiding shipping men getting ships in and out of ports safely and economically, not at warning of potential floods or estimating the frequency of such floods. However, the Technical Sub-Committee deemed LTI to be 'the best-informed body in the country on the subject of tides' and asked it to prepare a proposal for an inquiry into the causes and frequency of surges. The Institute proposed an initial inquiry limited to the Thames estuary, but from the start pointed out that a larger-scale inquiry covering the wider North Sea was likely to be necessary to answer the Sub-Committee's questions, as it was already known that surges were often generated further afield.[14] The mathematical research was designed to investigate 'the probability of the recurrence' of a tide as high as, or higher than, that experienced in early 1928, and to clarify 'the meteorological conditions which [were] most favourable to the production of storm effects on high water'.[15]

LTI's proposal for research focused on the Thames estuary was presented to the Technical Sub-Committee in late January by Arthur Doodson (1890–1968), one of the main scientists at LTI. The proposal was accepted, with the work to be done in association with the Meteorological Office and the Hydrographic Department of the Admiralty. The cost would be shared by LCC and PLA, who agreed to

[12] Gibbon, 'Report', 13 and 22–23.

[13] Ibid., 23–25; and draft minutes attached to letter from [unreadable signature] Chief Civil Assistant to Hydrographer to Doodson, 6 February 1928: Bidston Archive (hereafter BA), Box 16; 'London Floods Technical Sub-Committee 2nd meeting on the 3rd Feb 1928': BA, Box 16.

[14] Gibbon, 'Report', 26–27.

[15] A.T. Doodson, 'Report on Thames floods' and J.S. Dines, 'Meteorological conditions associated with high tides in the Thames', *Geophysical Memoir No.47 of the Meteorological Office* (1929).

each pay no more than £250.[16] The two agencies, who had both been accused in the media of not doing enough to prevent the flooding, were happy to take on the cost of this initial research, which was tightly defined as focusing on improving flood defences *in London*. Given the traditional definition of flood defence as a local issue, LCC and PLA could not protest against being asked to pay for this research, especially as refusing would no doubt have led to bad headlines in what was an election year for LCC. However, they and the rest of the conference made a point of recommending that if more research was needed beyond this initial work, central government ought to consider paying for it.[17] While accepting the initial work as of primarily local interest to be paid for locally, the conference laid the groundwork for future demands on central government for further work, staking out the boundaries for a debate that would last a decade.

LTI had made clear in their initial proposal that they thought a further, wider, inquiry would be necessary to fully answer the questions that had been set by the Technical Sub-Committee, and rather unsurprisingly, they came to the same conclusion at the end of their initial inquiry. While LTI had in fact increased the area under study to include the North Sea, they concluded that more work was necessary to answer fully the research questions.[18] More work was said to be needed to improve the warning system and also to provide further information regarding the necessary height of flood defences. The Technical Sub-Committee's final report recommended that 'the desirability of continued investigations should [...] be considered' and claimed that such investigations were of national interest, as storm surges affected a large area and travelled along the coast.[19] With this recommendation, the stage was set for local government actors to ask for further research to be done, framed as of national interest and thus to be paid for by national government.

Flood defence policy and the governance of London

These arguments for further research formed part of a wider debate during the 1930s on flood defence policy in London, especially who should control the policy and its implementation, which in turn linked to debates on how London should be governed. At this time LCC was responsible for setting the standard height of flood defences in London, though the riparian (riverside) owners of the land paid for the defences. Following the event in 1928, LCC was given further responsibilities related to the inspection of flood defences, but the 1879 Act which

---

[16] Gibbon, 'Report', 'Thames Floods B', *Times*, March 1 1928.

[17] Gibbon, 'Report', 24.

[18] 'Summary of report on the Thames flood', Doodson, summer 1928: BA, Box 16.

[19] Technically this was a meeting of only part of the sub-committee, but the report was presented as if it represented the whole sub-committee. 'Thames floods: Technical Sub-Committee's report', enclosure two to letter dated 10 August 1928 from MoH: London Metropolitan Archives (LMA), LCC/CL/MD/1/11.

had, for London, enshrined in law that flood defence was a local responsibility otherwise remained the same.[20] A long debate in the 1870s, before the 1879 Act was passed, had similarly focused on who should pay for and who should control flood defence. The debate had focused on whether flood defence should be a charge on the regional level of government (LCC's predecessor) or on the riparian owners of the land who had previously paid. Though the regional authority wanted to control flood defence policy they were not prepared to pay for building the defences, and in the end the costs remained a charge on local landowners, in the face of protests from the local authorities.[21] There was thus a history of disputes between the different layers of London government regarding who should pay for and control flood defence.

This history of disputes between different authorities was played out again following the 1928 event, when the question of how flood defence along the Thames should be coordinated was again raised and discussed by various conferences and committees until the mid-1930s.[22] Centralisation of power to one authority was generally favoured, but the question was which authority. Several regional-level authorities, LCC, PLA and the Thames Conservancy, wanted the coordinating powers. In the summer of 1934 LCC asked the Ministry of Health to make LCC the controlling authority.[23] The Ministry's much delayed response in early 1936 was that it was unable to do this because of the 'diversity of opinion' among local authorities on the 'principles to be embodied' by the legislation.[24] Clearly other authorities were not keen on LCC being given these powers. The idea of a coordinating flood prevention authority seems to have petered out after this.

The fate of the flood defence coordination authority was not at all unusual. The failure to create it was typical of attempts at further coordinating London government in the interwar period, especially where LCC wanted to take the lead. When a coordinating body was actually created, such as regarding transport or electricity, LCC did not have a strong role on it. Instead such bodies tended to take the form of public corporations managed by independent experts and with a strong influence from private industry.[25] Conflicts between different local authorities typified interwar London politics according to Young and Garside,

---

[20] *London County Council (General Powers) Act 1929 – Prevention of Floods.*

[21] Metropolitan Board of Works, 'Report of the Metropolitan Board of Works for the year 1877', *House of Commons Papers; Accounts and Papers* (1878). Metropolitan Board of Works, 'Report of the Metropolitan Board of Works for the year 1879', *House of Commons Papers; Accounts and Papers* (1880).

[22] Materials on these are held in LMA (folders LCC/CL/MD/1/8, LCC/CL/MD/1/115, and LCC/CL/GP/1/119) and in The National Archives (TNA) (e.g. folders HLG 51/39 and WORK 6/403).

[23] 'Report of the Departmental Committee on Thames Flood Prevention', Report of the General Purpose Committee, 16 July 1934: LMA, LCC/CL/GP/1/119.

[24] Francis to the Clerk of the LCC, 24 February 1936: TNA, HLG 51/39.

[25] J. Gillespie, 'Municipalism, monopoly and management: the demise of "Socialism in One County", 1918–1933', in A. Saint (ed.), *Politics and the People of London: The London County Council, 1889–1965* (London, 1989).

and Clapson.[26] What LCC saw as rationalisation and coordinated planning was often resisted by other local authorities, who resented what they saw as LCC's attempts at controlling them and extending its own powers. The problem of how to govern London was identified and discussed at the time, for example by William Robson, a Fabian protégé of the Webbs, who favoured a stronger regional-level authority, echoing Labour in their calls for a 'real Corporation of London'.[27] It has however been argued that LCC and the London Labour group increasingly accepted the status quo in the 1930s, no longer seeking to extend LCC's powers as much as had previously been done.[28] The case of the proposed flood prevention authority does not quite fit into this pattern. Instead this is a case of LCC, under both Municipal Reform (i.e. conservative) and Labour control, arguing strongly for increased powers for itself, though it failed to achieve them. Flood defence and how it should be coordinated was part of a wider set of acrimonious power struggles between different local and regional authorities in London; power struggles that were not resolved.

The second round of storm surge research

During these debates on flood defence policy one of the few things the London-based authorities agreed on was the proposed storm surge research. In their various reports and committees they repeatedly recommended that the second round of research should be done and, crucially, that it should be paid for by central government. Starting in 1930, LCC used these various recommendations to repeatedly, during several years, ask the Ministry of Health to instigate this further investigation by asking the Treasury to fund it.[29] While the Admiralty and LTI were also involved, it was LCC which repeatedly pushed the research. The proposed research did not have a tightly defined scope but emphasised the necessity for collecting more data from a wider area, including foreign ports.[30] In its contacts with the Ministry of Health, LCC claimed that more research was needed to know how high to build flood defences and framed the investigation as of national importance because storm surges affected a large area. Subsidiary

[26] M. Clapson, 'Localism, the London Labour Party and the LCC between the Wars', in A. Saint (ed.), *Politics and the People of London: The London County Council, 1889–1965* (London, 1989); K. Young and P.L. Garside, *Metropolitan London: Politics and Urban Change 1837–1981* (London, 1982).

[27] W.A. Robson, *The Government and Misgovernment of London* (London, 1939). He did not discuss flood defence. For more on him, see J. Davis, 'London's evolution – from parochialism to global metropolis', and M. Hebbert, 'William Robson, the Herbert Commission and "Greater London"', both in B. Kochan (ed.), *London Government – 50 Years of Debate: The Contribution of LSE's Greater London Group* (London, 2008).

[28] Gillespie, 'Municipalism', 124–5, Young and Garside, *Metropolitan London*, ch 7.

[29] LCC to the Secretary of the MoH, 15 August 1930: TNA, HLG 51/39.

[30] 'Data for the investigation of storm surges', appendix to Douglas (Hydrographer) to Doodson, 13 January 1931: BA, Box 120.

arguments for it to be of national concern were also employed, such as that even if the research would only assist London, the capital was of national importance, and also that London had already paid its due by LCC and PLA paying for the first round of research.[31]

Within the Ministry of Health, where a wide range of civil servants were involved with the case, the arguments were generally treated as potentially valid. For example, the Minister, Hilton Young, in 1933 thought the research would be 'useful' but could not offer any money for it out of the Ministry's ordinary budget.[32] Instead money had to be applied for separately from the Treasury. The Ministry of Health agreed sufficiently with LCC regarding the usefulness of the research to contact the Treasury regarding it at least four times between 1931 and 1936, but these requests for funding were continually refused. LCC's arguments were rejected once they reached the Treasury.

As Savage's analysis of the policy of Ministry of Health officials has shown, it emphasised financial 'efficiency' over expensive social policies in the interwar period, just as the 'Treasury view' at this time emphasised balanced national budgets, so it is unsurprising that both these departments resisted expenditure and in the end refused it.[33] Nobody, neither LCC nor the other local or regional authorities, the Ministry of Health, the Admiralty or the Treasury, wanted to spend their money on the investigation. However, what I am interested in here is the reasons given to refuse funding and how these refusals were framed. The rationale behind the refusals, which links the funding to general debates about the allocation of responsibility for flood defence, is what is interesting in this case.

Initially, the Treasury gave two reasons for refusing funding: it did not think the research was urgent, and there was a strict 'need for economy', which given the timing in 1931 after the financial crisis and cutbacks in government funding that year, is an unsurprising reply. In 1932 these reasons were repeated, with the addition that the Treasury saw this as a local matter, not a national issue, and that therefore it should be paid for by local authorities and not central government. According to the Treasury, it did not matter that many local authorities over a

---

[31] Good summaries of the complicated debates are provided by the memo on 'North Sea Surge', attached to 'Minute sheet' by W.A. Ross, 2 May 1933, and the report 'Thames Flood Prevention – North Sea Surges – Further Investigations' to the General Purposes Committee, 4 May 1933, both in TNA, HLG 51/39. This folder contains material on the Ministry of Health side. There is also further material on the LCC side in the LMA (folders LCC/CL/MD/1/8, LCC/CL/MD/1/11, LCC/CL/MD/1/115, LCC/CL/MD/2/53, LCC/CL/GP/1/119). It has not been possible to locate any Treasury files.

[32] Armer to the Clerk of LCC, 6 May 1933: TNA, HLG 51/39.

[33] P. Clarke, 'The Treasury's analytical model of the British economy between the wars', in M.O. Furner and B. Supple (eds.), *The State and Economic Knowledge: The American and British Experiences* (Cambridge, 1990); G.C. Peden, *The Treasury and British Public Policy, 1906–1959* (Oxford, 2000); G. Savage, *The Social Construction of Expertise: The English Civil Service and Its Influence, 1919–1939* (London, 1996).

wide area were involved: it was still something the local authorities should deal with. A similar response was given in 1934. In 1936 Ministry of Health officials again contacted the Treasury and again were told no money was forthcoming. The minute made after this meeting points towards a key underlying reason for the lack of Treasury support. They still did not see the issue as a national one, but more importantly did not want to set a precedent: 'The argument, if conceded for the cost of the enquiry, could or possibly would also be applied to the consequential work on defences in the Thames and elsewhere.'[34] If this investigation was accepted as a national responsibility this was thought to imply that flood defence could be seen as a national government responsibility, instead of the responsibility of the riverside or coastal landowner and the local authorities as it had traditionally been, and the Treasury did not want this. It did not want to pay for the building of flood defences. While LCC claimed to be simply asking for patronage for a small scientific investigation, the Treasury saw the request as the beginning of a wider request for funding of flood defences. It was determined to stick to the general principle that flood defence remain a local responsibility, so the research also had to remain a local responsibility.

It is not clear from the sources whether LCC knew the Treasury's view on this (they do not appear to have been told formally, but may of course have heard of it informally), nor if they had any plans to widen their appeal towards flood defence more generally if this appeal had been successful. A year and a half later, in June 1937 the positions were described as a 'deadlock of policy'.[35] At this point, however, LCC had a change of mind. On the chief engineer's suggestion it was decided to ask LTI if it was willing to still do the investigation at the previously agreed price of £1,100 while promises of money from various coastal local authorities were also collected.[36] The only reason given for this change of mind was 'the undoubted necessity' of the investigation and the 'continued refusal of H.M. Government to defray the small expenditure involved'.[37] I have found no evidence of any other reasons than that LCC simply gave up on the Government ever giving in on this issue. This issue was part of the often fraught relationship LCC had with central government – even the official history of LCC, published in 1939, described its relationship with central government as frequently dominated by fights.[38] After the protracted debates, LCC gave in and decided they wanted the investigation more than they wanted government money for it. At least for now, the responsibility for flood defence had been firmly assigned

[34] Minute sheet, Accountant-General S.C. Alford, 18 February 1936: TNA, HLG 51/39.

[35] Minute sheet on Thames Flood Prevention, Note to the Clerk of the Council, signed A w B (?), 22 June 1937: LMA, LCC/CL/MD/1/115.

[36] Frank Peirson (Chief Engineer) to Doodson, 16 August 1937: BA, Box 120.

[37] Extract of Minutes from General Purposes Committee, 'Storm surges in the North Sea. Reply to memorandum of 11th May, 1936', 8 July 1937: LMA, LCC/CL/MD/1/115.

[38] R.W. Bell and G.J. Gibbon, *History of the London County Council 1889–1939* (London, 1939), 581–90.

to the local/regional level and the Treasury's view on flood defence as a local issue had prevailed.

In early 1938 the research got going, with funding from LCC, PLA and a number of other coastal local authorities.[39] The war interrupted the work, but not before LTI had fulfilled a request from their contact at the Hydrographic Department of the Admiralty in 1940 for a surge prediction formula for the continental coast. These predictive formulae used methods developed as part of the LCC research.[40] After the war, the work for LCC was picked up and LTI's final report was sent to LCC in February 1947.[41]

The publication of the report became a complicated affair. Out of the blue, the Royal Navy Scientific Service put in a request to LCC on behalf of the UK and US Navies to be allowed to copy the report, which was granted without consulting LTI.[42] Its only full copy of the report, which had been sent to LCC, was lent to the Royal Naval Scientific Service, which in turn gave it to the American Embassy. After many twists and turns, with versions of the report, its contents and corrections sent hither and thither, the report was reproduced in Washington, D.C., as a Hydrographic Office publication.[43] The publication of the report seems to have been caught up in a wider US-led exchange of scientific information between the UK and the US naval authorities that was taking place at this time.[44]

The work done for the Admiralty during the Second World War and the American interest in LTI's report on the second investigation indicate a shift away from local authority patronage of storm surge science towards military patronage.[45] However, the military interest in storm surge science during and after the Second World War was soon overtaken by state patronage. In 1953, after the

[39] See documents in LMA, LCC/CL/MD/1/115.

[40] Doodson to the Clerk to the Council, 16 October 1941: BA, Box 120 and the attached 'Report on the present state of work on storm surges in North Sea'.

[41] Doodson to the Chief Engineer, 20 March 1946: BA, Box 120; and Doodson to the Deputy Chief Engineer, 1 February 1947: BA, Box 120.

[42] 'Storm surges in the North Sea, Housing Committee, Report by the Chief Engineer', 15 May 1948: LMA, LCC/CL/MD/1/115.

[43] See correspondence between 1947 and 1949 in BA, Box 120 and 130, and also in LMA folder LCC/CL/MD/1/115. The report is R.H. Corkan, *Storm Surges in the North Sea*, 2 vols. (Hydrographic Office Misc. 15072, Washington D.C., 1948).

[44] For example, the file TNA, ADM 116/5670, contains lists of a large number of scientific reports that were exchanged between the UK and the US.

[45] Work in the US on the history of oceanography has found the military to have been the dominant patron of oceanography. LTI is a case that complicates this story of heavy military patronage of oceanography. While LTI had clear links to the navy, through the Hydrographic Department, a large part of its funding and patronage came from the shipping industry, and as we have seen here local authorities were important patrons for storm surge science. See J.D. Hamblin, *Oceanographers and the Cold War: Disciples of Marine Science* (London, 2005), G.E. Weir, *Ocean in Common: American Naval Officers, Scientists, and the Ocean Environment* (College Station, Texas, 2001), S. Schlee, *A History of Oceanography: The Edge of an Unfamiliar World* (London, 1973).

East Coast Floods in which over 300 people died, the British state became firmly involved with coastal defence and quickly became the main financial patron of storm surge science, with funding and research direction provided by a specialised advisory committee under the Ministry of Agriculture and Fisheries. With this, the patronage of storm surge science shifted towards central government.

Conclusion

What I have shown here is that this transfer of patronage to national government was a contested process, without an obvious or straightforward outcome. It was set amid wider debates and wider power struggles between different layers of government and different local and regional authorities. The funding of storm surge science in the 1930s was not just about the funding of a small piece of research, but had larger implications in terms of general flood defence policy and who should pay for building defences. The second round of research was delayed as it was caught up in debates between local, regional and national government regarding the control of flood policy and funding of flood defences, with central government allocating responsibility for it to local and regional authorities, while these contested this allocation.

5.   Rediscovering the Thames

Gustav Milne

Thames Discovery Programme

The Thames foreshore is rich in archaeological sites, a neglected and largely untapped reservoir of research potential, in spite of the work of such pioneers as Ivor Noel-Hume, whose 1955 book *Treasure in the Thames* clearly set out the archaeological significance of the inter-tidal zone. Regrettably, all these sites are being gradually (or rapidly) destroyed. The Thames Discovery Programme is very concerned about the progressive erosion of these archaeological sites and features, and in response, we are training up a committed team of Londoners who will regularly survey and monitor the fate of some 20 key sites on the foreshore, not just during the present 3-year Heritage Lottery Fund supported project, but for perpetuity. We have called this group the Foreshore Recording and Observation Group, or FROG.

The Thames Discovery Programme is hosted by the Thames Estuary Partnership, based at the Environment Institute, University College London: we employ a small but dedicated team of professional archaeologists and an Outreach Officer, based at Museum of London's London Archaeological Archive and Research Centre. These are Nathalie Cohen our Team Leader, Elliot Wragg, Survey Officer, Lorna Richardson, Outreach Officer, and we also called upon the services of Dr Stuart Brookes as IT/ GIS consultant, as well as Dr Sue Harrington.[1]

Our progress is monitored by a steering group, with representation from various institutions, notably the Thames Explorer Trust, English Heritage, Environment Agency, Museum of London, UCL Institute of Archaeology, UCL Public Engagement Unit, the Port of London Authority, University of East London and the Council for British Archaeology. Most importantly, we were most fortunate to be awarded a three-year grant from the Heritage Lottery Fund (2008–2011).

There are four main strands to the project:

a) the new, high-precision BETA survey of key selected sites;
b) the training programme for over 200 new FROG members, incorporating classroom sessions, hands-on recording work on site, as well as a series of week-long Summer Seasons on the foreshore;
c) a wide-ranging Outreach Programme involving the organisation or attendance at a series of river-related events, seminars and conferences throughout the year, at a variety of locations;

---

[1] http://www.thamesdiscovery.org/; http://www.thamesweb.com/

d) the RIVERPEDIA community-research programme, facilitating studies by the FROG members on Thames-based themes.

Building on the work of the Thames Archaeological Survey

Running broadly west to east through the Thames Valley from Teddington to the North Sea are exposed sections through the complex sequence of deposits and features on both banks of the river. The Thames foreshore forms the longest archaeological site in the London region, but is only exposed at low tide, and is continuously under threat from erosion. Although the Thames is well-known as a provenance for archaeological finds, the foreshore in central London had never been subjected to a systematic survey prior to the work of the *Thames Archaeological Survey*. This was set up informally in 1993, working from University College London (UCL), but was formally established in 1995 when Mike Webber was appointed as Survey Officer to conduct a pilot study of five sites to assess the potential of a wider investigation. This work was funded by English Heritage, with support from UCL and from the Museum of London. The findings were of such significance that a more comprehensive survey of the tidal foreshore within the Greater London area was then set up, funded by the Environment Agency and English Heritage, again with substantial support from the Museum of London and UCL.

This 'Alpha Survey' took three years, and covered the majority of the tideway on both banks of the Thames in over 150 *Survey Zones*, concentrating on the Thames west of the Barrier. It produced an impressive inventory of features and sites, the locations of which are now entered on the Greater London Sites and Monuments Record (GLHER).[2] The work involved up to three Survey Officers (one of whom was Nathalie Cohen), recording features alongside foreshore teams drawn from a range of local societies and university groups, an exercise in community archaeology on a London-wide scale. The finds included substantial tracts of prehistoric deposits including peat, silts and the remains of submerged forests, such as the extensive site at Erith; at least one Bronze Age bridge or jetty structure at Vauxhall; several pile-built fish traps, most of which were of Saxon or medieval date, such as the large feature at Chelsea; the remains of jetties, causeways and landing stages of sixteenth to nineteenth-century date; the footings of Putney's eighteenth-century bridge; many boats, barge and ships fragments, including the evidence of several foreshore ship-building and ship-breaking yards.

Prior to the 1990s, many were of the opinion that objects found on the foreshore were unstratified and/or were thrown into the river for ritual purposes, and that the foreshore itself was a conglomeration of disturbed deposits containing no effective archaeologically-viable stratification. These assumptions were finally

---

[2] Searchable via the Archaeology Data Service website: <http://ads.ahds.ac.uk/catalogue/collections/blurbs/272.cfm>

corrected by the work of the Thames Archaeological Survey which unequivocally demonstrated that:

a) the London foreshore does indeed incorporate stratified archaeological sites;

b) many foreshore finds are eroding out of such stratified deposits (i.e. not all ritually-deposited);

c) those foreshore features are subject to continuing erosion: indeed, they are only visible on the surface of the foreshore when they are in the process of being destroyed by the daily scour of the tidal Thames.

The new Thames Discovery Programme

When the new survey programme commenced in 2008, it soon became clear that the foreshore had changed dramatically since the 1990s: features which had been noted previously were no longer there, while a plethora of new features amply confirmed the thesis that foreshore erosion is accelerating. TDP is therefore undertaking high-precision contoured surveys of 20 key sites, these surveys forming the basis of all future recording work. Our FROG team will then survey and resurvey those sites annually, reporting their findings to the GLHER.

However, our work does not end there: these sites will also form the focus for community research projects on a range of riverine themes looking at changes in river levels, tidal head, riverbank encroachment and archaeological evidence of flood events, often evident in the heightening of river walls. Then there is the changing use of the river, and evidence for related social economic and technological change. One theme that is attracting particular interest is the change for sail- to steam-powered shipping in the nineteenth century, a revolution that had a major impact on all of the maritime communities along the Thames.

From sail to steam

Two examples will serve to show how we use our foreshore survey work to focus on wider research questions. The change from wind-powered wooden ships to steam-powered metal-hulled vessels is illustrated by two recent projects, one looking at a ship-breakers yard where the venerable HMS Duke of Wellington was broken up at Charlton, and the survey of the launch site of Brunel's monster steam ship, the Great Eastern at Millwall.

In 2008, a stack of large ship timbers was observed on the foreshore on the site of Castle's Shipbreaking Yard. The timbers were recorded in more detail in 2009, and Eliott Wragg was able to identify some of them as being derived from HMS Duke of Wellington, which, when launched in 1854, was the largest wooden warship of its type, the 131-gun flag ship of the Royal Navy. But in military terms, it was rendered obsolete almost immediately, following the launch at Bow Creek of the ironclad HMS Warrior in 1860, a radically-new nautical weapon. HMS Duke of Wellington was a throwback to the days of HMS Victory, the era of wooden sailing ships and broadside gunnery, and it was decommissioned and eventually broken up at the turn of the century. The Thames had long housed communities with the skills to build such large vessels, fit them with masts, ropes and sails, and to man them on their long and arduous voyages. That long history of expertise, like HMS Duke of Wellington itself, was suddenly rendered obsolete. Our sorry stack of timbers thus commemorates not just that vessel, but also the now-vanished Thames-based crafts, trades and skills that such once supported such vessels.

On the opposite bank of the river at Millwall, the Thames Discovery team have been recording the remains of the two slipways used in 1859 during the infamous sideways launch of the 200m-long SS Great Eastern, the largest steam-powered metal-hulled vessel built on the Thames. Work began on the construction of this leviathan in 1854 (ironically the same year as the launch of HMS Duke of Wellington), and the launch proved just as much a challenge for Isambard Kingdom Brunel as the construction itself. However, in January 1859 – after several previous attempts – the vessel was finally hauled down the slipways into the river at high tide. In 1984, part of one slipway was revealed during building works on dry land near Napier Road E14. Taken together with our new survey of the remains of the two 37m-wide slipways just visible on the foreshore, we can now accurately locate the precise position where the vessel was built from 1854–8, when it attracted many astonished onlookers. The TDP team are now trying to facilitate a major outreach project to establish a 200m-long waterfront 'park' in the shape of the Great Eastern, complete with its five funnels and six masts. This could serve as a new Thames-Path landmark for London. It would be a monument for Millwall and its maritime expertise, standing as it did at the cutting edge of nautical technology.

Blitz on the river

The final example of foreshore survey is throwing light on a previously untold story of the London Blitz, through its examination of repairs to the river wall made in the 1940s as a result of bomb strikes. We have all heard of the famous 'Dam Busters' raid in 1943, when the RAF's 617 squadron breached two dams in the Ruhr valley – Germany's industrial heartland – and consequently flooded a vast area, drowning over a thousand souls. But London is low-lying and thus very vulnerable to flooding: what if the Luftwaffe had breached our river walls during the Blitz, and inundated acres of our own conurbation? What if they could flood the underground, where so many Londoners sought refuge? We all know that our flood defences were not compromised during the dark days of the Blitz: but it is not widely appreciated how close we came to such a catastrophe. Unpublished records in the London Metropolitan Archives have revealed that the river wall was hit no less than 121 times between 1940 and 1945, but not one of these potentially serious breaches resulted in a major flood.

It is now possible to show that the answer lies in very detailed forward planning on the part of the LCC's Chief Engineer, Sir Pierson Frank. He arrived in London to take up his new post in the aftermath of the 1928 flood that saw the river wall breached and overtopped, with many properties flooded and lives lost. He was thus fully aware of the potential threat the Thames posed to London in peace-time, all the more so during aerial bombardment. Before the Blitz began, he therefore commissioned a survey of the most vulnerable riverside sites, grading them from I (the worst) to III, and circulated the data to each of the borough engineers in the LCC area. He also sent a separate letter stating the days and times of the highest anticipated spring tides for the year, i.e. specifying the actual time at which the defences were at their most vulnerable. Taken together, these two documents, if they fell into enemy hands, could have proved catastrophic: what if the Luftwaffe had chosen to concentrate their HE bombs on the weakest sections of the river wall just one or two hours before an exceptionally high tide? Well aware of the dreadful significance of this information, the tide charts were sent to just one named officer in each borough, but only after the name, address and nationality of that officer was checked.

While temporary works were being instated to serve as a new line of flood defence in the worst areas, he selected four sites as depots for large stores of sandbags, timber and tarpaulin, so that the most vulnerable areas could be rapidly supported in the event of a major bomb-strike on a Grade I river wall. His careful planning paid off, as study of the two surviving Log Books show. The first records 84 incidents from 1940 to May 1941 (the Blitz), the second lists a further 37 incidents up to 24 March 1945, covering the period of the 'Baby Blitz' and the V1 and V2 rocket attacks. But not one of these potential disasters resulted in a major flood event

All in all, the highly organised work of the Chief Engineer's team deserves plaudits: we have not modelled what might have happened if just one of those major breaches had not been successfully checked: given the destruction caused downstream by the floods in 1947 and upstream by the floods in 1953, then London surely does have a debt of gratitude to pay to all those involved. Perhaps now, some seventy years after the event, we can at last publically recognise their real achievement.

As part of that process of recognition, the Thames Discovery Programme team are now recording the evidence for those river wall repairs, where they can still be identified. The crucial temporary repairs, conducted within hours or days of the initial strike, were the work of Frank's teams, but the 'permanent' repairs were the responsibility of the owner of that section of river wall, and thus vary in quality. We have, for example, recorded two repairs of very different nature within 200m of each other: at Bishops Park, Fulham (breached 16 October 1940) the repaired section of the river wall is almost indistinguishable from the rest of the embankment walling, save for the re-set drains and iron balustrade work. In marked contrast, the work undertaken at Craven Cottage, by the then impoverished

Fulham Football Club, was not completed until a year after the initial strike (26 November 1940), and is easily identifiable as shuttered concrete infill above the shattered remnants of the earlier brick-built river wall.

Conclusion

At the end of the three-year period of support provided by the Heritage Lottery Fund, it is hoped that the TDP will be broadly self-sustaining. Londoners will have their own London-wide Community Archaeology Project in which they can all actively participate, initially to monitor the pace of erosion of selected sites exposed on the foreshore. But we also want to extend that work, utilising our foreshore studies to provide a physical focus for further research and to provide raw data on a host of Thames-related themes. By getting people's hands dirty and their curiosity aroused, we hope to provide a stimulus for Londoners to undertake their own research on London's River, whether on the foreshore, with a museum collection or in an archive centre.

Consolidated bibliography of secondary works

Baker, T.F.T. (ed.), *A History of the County of Middlesex* (Victoria County History) vol. 11 (London, 1998).

Barron, C.M, *London in the Later Middle Ages* (Oxford, 2004).

Bell, R.W. and Gibbon, G.J., *History of the London County Council 1889–1939* (London, 1939).

Biddulph, E. and Hardy, A. *et al.* in preparation, Oxford Archaeology monograph on Roman and Saxon Northfleet.

Blatherwick, S. and Bluer, R., *Great Houses, Moats and Mills on the South Bank of the Thames: Medieval and Tudor Southwark and Rotherhithe* (Museum of London Archaeology Monograph 47, 2009).

Bowler, E.E.M. , 'The reclamation and land-use of the Thames marshes of North West Kent', Ph.D. thesis, University of London (1968).

Brazell, J.H., *London Weather* (Meteorological Office publication 783, London, 1968).

Brigham, T., 'The Thames and Southwark waterfront in the Roman Period', in B. Watson, T. Brigham, and T. Dyson, *London Bridge 2000 years of a River Crossing* (MoLAS Monograph 8, 2001), 12–27.

Carlsson, A. 'What is a storm: severe weather and public life in Britain in January 1928', in V. Jankovic and C. Barboza (eds.), *Weather, Local Knowledge and Everyday Life: Issues in Integrated Climate Studies* (Rio de Janeiro, 2009).

Cioc, M., *The Rhine: An Eco-Biography, 1815–2000* (Seattle, 2002).

M. Clapson, 'Localism, the London Labour Party and the LCC between the Wars', in A. Saint (ed.), *Politics and the People of London: The London County Council, 1889–1965* (London, 1989).

Clarke, P., 'The Treasury's analytical model of the British economy between the wars', in M.O. Furner and B. Supple (eds.), *The State and Economic Knowledge: The American and British Experiences* (Cambridge, 1990).

C.M., *The Laws of Sewers* (London 1762).

Cockayne, E., *Hubbub: Filth, Noise and Stench in England 1600–1770* (London, 2007).

Corkan, R.H., *Storm Surges in the North Sea*, 2 vols. (Hydrographic Office Misc. 15072, Washington D.C., 1948).

Darlington, I., 'The London Commissioners of Sewers and their Records', in F. Ranger (ed.), *Prisca Munimenta* (London, 1973).

Davis, J., 'London's evolution – from parochialism to global metropolis', in B. Kochan (ed.), *London Government – 50 Years of Debate: The Contribution of LSE's Greater London Group* (London, 2008).

Dines, J.S., 'Meteorological conditions associated with high tides in the Thames', *Geophysical Memoir No.47 of the Meteorological Office* (1929).

Doodson, A.T., 'Report on Thames floods', *Geophysical Memoir No.47 of the Meteorological Office* (1929).

Dugdale, W., *The History of Imbanking and Draining* (2nd edn., London, 1777).

Faulkener, N. with Davis, S., 'Water-power in medieval Greenwich', *Current Archaeology* 236 (2009), 30–35.

Farmer, D.L., 'Prices and wages', in E. Miller (ed.), *The Agrarian History of England and Wales* vol. 3, *1348–1500* (Cambridge 1991), 431–525.

Fitz Stephen, W., *Norman London* (New York, 1990).

Galloway, J.A., 'Storm flooding, coastal defence and land use around the Thames estuary and tidal river, *c*.1250-1450', *Journal of Medieval History* 30 (2009), 1–18.

Galloway, J.A. and Potts, J., 'Marine flooding in the Thames estuary and tidal river *c*.1250–1450: impact and response', *Area* 39 (2007), 370–9.

Gillespie, J., 'Municipalism, monopoly and management: the demise of "Socialism in One County", 1918–1933', in A. Saint (ed.), *Politics and the People of London: The London County Council, 1889–1965* (London, 1989).

Golinski, J., *British Weather and the Climate of Enlightenment* (Chicago, 2007).

Goodburn, D., 'Woods and woodland; carpenters and carpentry', in G. Milne (ed.), *Timber Building Techniques in London c.900–1400* (London and Middlesex Archaeological Society Special Paper No. 15, 1992).

Goodburn, D., 'Timber studies', in J. Hill and A. Woodger (eds.), *Excavations at 72–75 Cheapside/ 83–93 Queen Street*, MoLAS Archaeological Studies 2 (1999).

Gottschalk, E., *Stormvloeden en Rivieroverstromingen in Nederland,* 3 vols. (Assen, 1971–78).

Hamblin, J.D., *Oceanographers and the Cold War: Disciples of Marine Science* (London, 2005).

Hanley, J.G., 'The Metropolitan Commissioners of Sewers and the law, 1812–1847', *Urban History* 33 (2006).

Hargrave, F., *The Law of Sewers* (London, 1732).

Hasted, E., *The History and Topographical Survey of the County of Kent: Volume 2* (1797), 203–63.

Hebbert, M. 'William Robson, the Herbert Commission and "Greater London"', in B. Kochan (ed.), *London Government – 50 Years of Debate: The Contribution of LSE's Greater London Group* (London, 2008).

H. Humpherus, *History of the Origin and Progress of the Company of Watermen and Lightermen of the river Thames with Numerous Historical Notes,* vol. 2 (Wakefield, 1981).

Inwood, S., *A History of London* (London, 2000).

Jefferson-Smith, P., 'Before Bazalgette: the Surrey and Kent Commission of Sewers, 1800–1847', *Transactions of the Newcomen Society*, 74 (2004).

Keene, D., 'Issues of water in medieval London', *Urban History* 21 (2008), 161–79.

de Kraker, A.M.J., 'Reconstruction of storm frequency in the North Sea area of the preindustrial period, 1400–1625 and the connection with reconstructed time series of temperatures', *History of Meteorology* 2 (2005), 51–70.

Lamb, H.H., *Climate, History and the Modern World* (London, 1982).

Lavery, S. and Donovan, B., 'Flood risk management in the Thames Estuary looking ahead 100 years', *Philosophical Transactions of the Royal Society*, Series A, vol. 363, no. 1831 (2005), 1455–74.

Lowe, E.J., *Natural Phenomena and Chronology of the Seasons* (London, 1870).

McRobie, A., Spencer, T. and Gerritsen, H., 'The Big Flood: North Sea Storm Surge', *Philosophical Transactions of the Royal Society*, Series A, vol. 363, no. 1831 (2005), 1263–70.

Marsden, P., *Ships of the Port of London Twelfth to Seventeenth Centuries AD* (English Heritage, Archaeological Report 5, 1996).

Merriman, R.B., *Life and Letters of Thomas Cromwell*, vol I: *Life, Letters to 1535* (Oxford, 1902), 324–5.

Milne, A., *London's Drowning* (London, 1982)

Milne, G., *The Port of Medieval London* (Stroud, 2003).

Milne, G. and Milne, C., *Medieval Waterfront Development at Trig Lane, London* (London and Middlesex Archaeological Society Special Paper No. 5, 1982).

Mirrlees, S.T.A, 'The Thames floods of January 7th', *The Meteorological Magazine* (1928).

Nienhuis, P.H., *Environmental History of the Rhine-Meuse Delta* (New York, 2008).

Noel-Hume, I., *Treasure in the Thames* (London, 1955).

Peden, G.C., *The Treasury and British Public Policy, 1906–1959* (Oxford, 2000).

Porter, D.H., *The Thames Embankment, Environment, Technology, and Society in Victorian London* (Akron, Ohio, 1998).

Powell, W.R. (ed.), *A History of the County of Essex* (Victoria County History), vol. 6 (London, 1973).

Rhatz, P. and Meeson, R., *An Anglo-Saxon Watermill at Tamworth* (Council for British Archaeology Research Report No. 83, 1992).

Robson, W.A., *The Government and Misgovernment of London* (London, 1939).

Rocque, J., *A Plan of the Cities of London and Westminster, and Borough of Southwark; with the Contiguous Buildings* (1746).

Sabine, E.L., 'Butchering in mediaeval London', *Speculum* 8 (1933), 335–53.

Savage, G., *The Social Construction of Expertise: The English Civil Service and Its Influence, 1919–1939* (London, 1996).

Schlee, S., *A History of Oceanography: The Edge of an Unfamiliar World* (London, 1973).

Sturman, W.M., 'Barking abbey: a study in its external and internal administration from the conquest to the dissolution', PhD. thesis, University of London (1961).

Sunderland, D., '"A monument to defective administration"? The London Commissioners of Sewers in the early nineteenth century', *Urban History* 26, (1999).

Ungar, S., 'The rise and (relative) decline of global warming as a social problem', *The Sociological Quarterly* 33, no. 4 (1992).

Ward, J.P., 'The taming of the Thames: reading the river in the seventeenth century', *Huntington Library Quarterly* 71 (2008), 55–75.

Webb, S. and B., *English Local Government from the Revolution to the Municipal Corporations Act, Volume IV: Statutory Authorities for Special Purposes* (London, 1922).

Weir, G.E., *Ocean in Common: American Naval Officers, Scientists, and the Ocean Environment* (College Station, Texas, 2001).

Wheeler, A., *The Tidal Thames: The History of a River and its Fishes* (London, 1979).

Young, K. and Garside, P.L., *Metropolitan London: Politics and Urban Change 1837–1981* (London, 1982).

Lightning Source UK Ltd.
Milton Keynes UK
UKHW030714271120
374207UK00006B/382